Landscape Fiber Painting

It's Not Paint, It's Fabric

Heidi K. Heuerman

Landscape Fiber Painting

It's not Paint, it's Fabric

www.ArtzPress.com

Library of Congress Control Number: 2014907082

ISBN: 978-0-692-20120-6

1. Crafts & Hobbies / Textiles

2. Machine Appliqué

3. Fabric Pictures

QUANTITY PURCHASES: Companies, professional groups, clubs, and other organizations may qualify for special terms when ordering quantities of this title. For information

e-mail info@artzpress.com

This book is printed in the United States of America.

Dedication

This book is dedicated to my mom, Diane Peterson, for all her support and encouragement. Thank you!

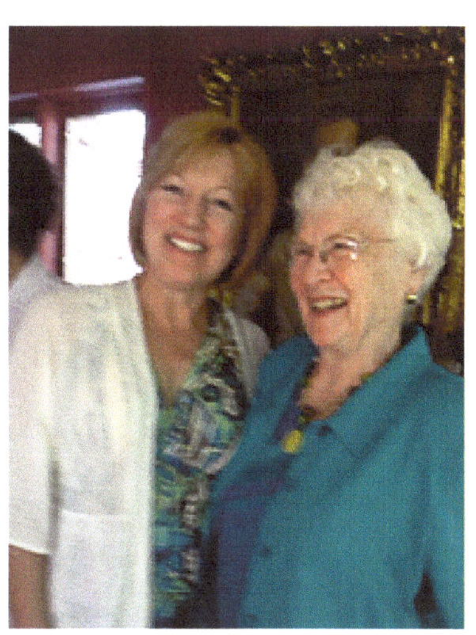

Acknowledgments

I want to thank my children, Rachel and Mark for all their thoughts and ideas for my pictures. A big thank you goes to my parents, Colin and Diane and my sisters Amy and Inga for all their never-ending support. A special note of thanks to all the ladies at Pearls, our special knitting/crochet group. And all my P.E.O. friends in Maryville Missouri and Sheridan Wyoming. Thank you all!

Contents

About the Author

Heidi Heuerman started sewing when she was eight years old. She started young, making Holly Hobby dolls, then Barbie clothes, funky jewelry, clothes, and home décor trinkets. While earning her degree in Human Resource Sciences at Colorado State University, she took a painting class, and loved it. Years later, while trying to find a way to combine her love of painted landscapes and sewing she started creating fiber paintings.

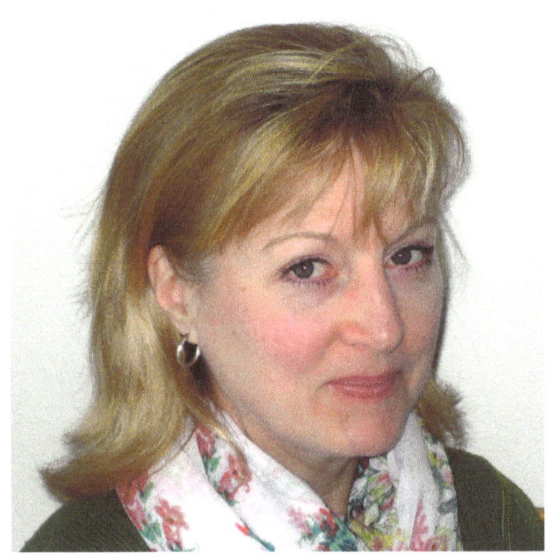

Heuerman's works have been displayed in several galleries and collections across the United States. She took top honors at State and National awards for her fiber and quilted arts.

Heidi lives with her husband, Wayne and two children in Maryville, Missouri. In their spare time, they enjoy taking road-trips, learning about local history and seeing new and interesting sights. She especially enjoys her visits to the mountains of Wyoming, always looking for a new fiber painting idea.

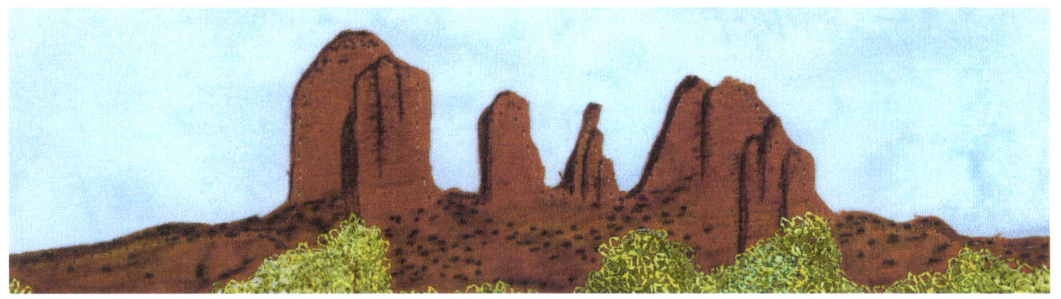

Preface

I have so many pretty pictures of places I've been, or pictures that family members have taken, but I didn't want more photographs hanging in my house. I wanted something different. I'd been sewing traditional quilts, clothes and crafty things for many years, but I wanted to make something more creative and be able to combine my love of landscape paintings with my sewing. That's when I started making my landscape fiber paintings. By the term "fiber paintings" I mean the medium can include anything that has to do with fiber; fabrics, threads, netting, embroidery floss, and beyond. Sometimes I'll also add some acrylic and fabric paint and permanent markers to bring my pictures to life. I have various pieces displayed in Wyoming, Colorado, Washington, Iowa and Missouri. And wherever I am, I hear people ask the same thing: "how do you do that?" That is why I decided to write this book.

The world of fiber art is amazing! There are so many creative ways to use fabrics and fibers. This is just one of them. I love the feel of the fabrics, and all the wonderful colors. It is so much fun to be able to recreate a favorite photograph into a three-dimensional work of art, and be able to bring the feeling of that special place to life. Memories come alive when recreating the details of that special place. As I'm adding the details of a piece it brings back memories of the temperature, the smells, the sounds, the light, and who was with me at the time.

I hope you enjoy learning about the art of fiber painting; I know it has enriched my life considerably!

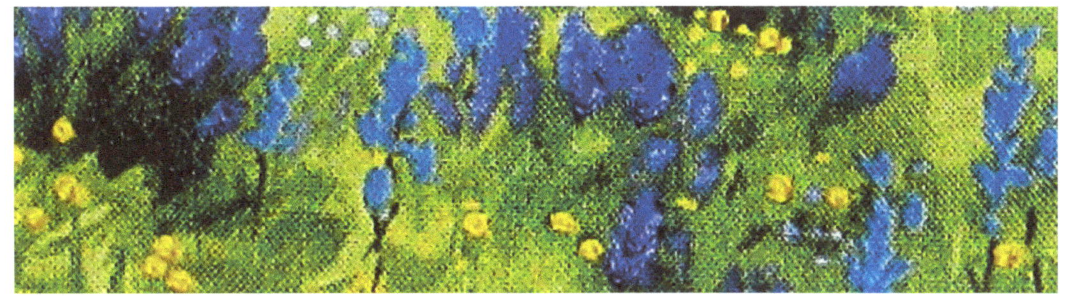

Introduction

Do you want to experience the world of Fiber Arts, but feel overwhelmed? Do you want to try to make a landscape fiber painting, but don't know where to begin? Are you new to sewing? In this book, I will take that overwhelming feeling away. You'll learn how to select a good inspirational photo to use for a landscape fiber painting. You will make your "canvas." You'll also learn the different stitches used to create the effects you want. You will learn how to use paints and pens to get the look and feel you want. And you'll learn how to finish your piece so that you can proudly display your work of art.

If you're new to sewing, that's okay. Creating fiber paintings parallels nature. You'll rarely need to be able to sew a straight line because nature rarely has straight lines. This book will take you through the complete process of making landscape fiber paintings. And along the way, you'll find tips and hints to take the scariness out of this type of fiber art. So turn the page and let's begin.

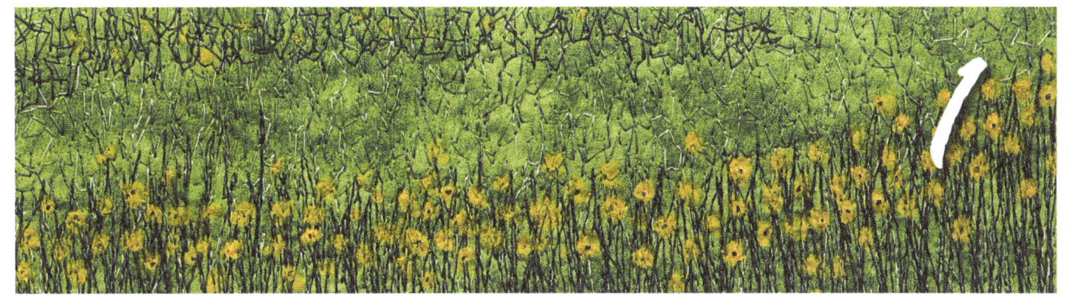

Things to have on Hand

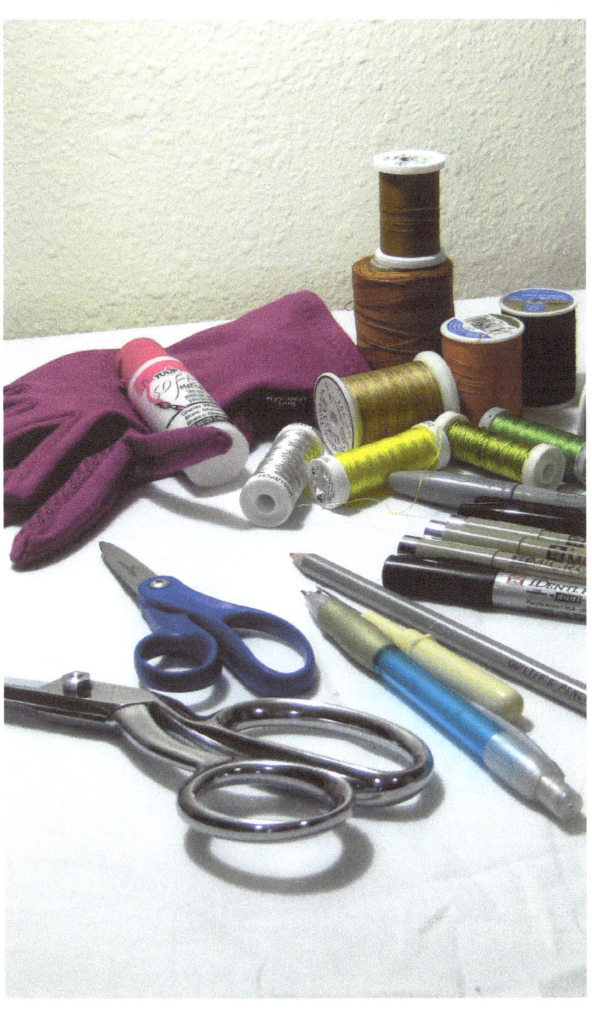

Here is a list of things to have on hand:

- A Sewing machine with the capability to drop the feed dogs and use a darning presser foot, or free-motion capabilities.
- Needle(s) for your machine. I use Universal or Microtex in size 80/12. You want a needle that won't leave large holes in your fabrics.
- Fabrics that have a high thread count or are tightly woven. They hold up much better to all the stitching you'll be doing.
- Threads in various colors that go with your picture. I use threads made out of cotton, polyester, silk and rayon, plus a clear one to attach your fabrics to your canvas.
- A fusible interfacing that is fairly light-weight, but will give your canvas some stability.

- ☐ Muslin, to use for the backing of your canvas.
- ☐ A light-weight spray adhesive to baste your fabric pieces to your canvas before stitching. I like to use 505 Adhesive Spray.
- ☐ An Iron
- ☐ Scissors, I use a large pair and a small, rounded tip pair.
- ☐ A Design Wall or Design Board is handy.
- ☐ Spray Starch. I like Mary Ellen's Best Press. It doesn't leave white flakes behind, plus it smells nice.
- ☐ A Pencil for marking your canvas and drawing the pattern pieces for your picture.
- ☐ Tracing Paper is handy but not necessary. I like to use it to make pattern pieces for the different fabrics. You can see through it which is very helpful.
- ☐ Pre-cut Mat Boards for preparing your canvas and for viewing your artwork along the process of making it. I have a natural colored 11" x 14" mat that I can reuse for making various pictures.
- ☐ Quilters Gloves can come in handy because they give you more control when holding the canvas while doing the free-motion sewing.
- ☐ A Seam Ripper, to help pull threads to the back of your picture.

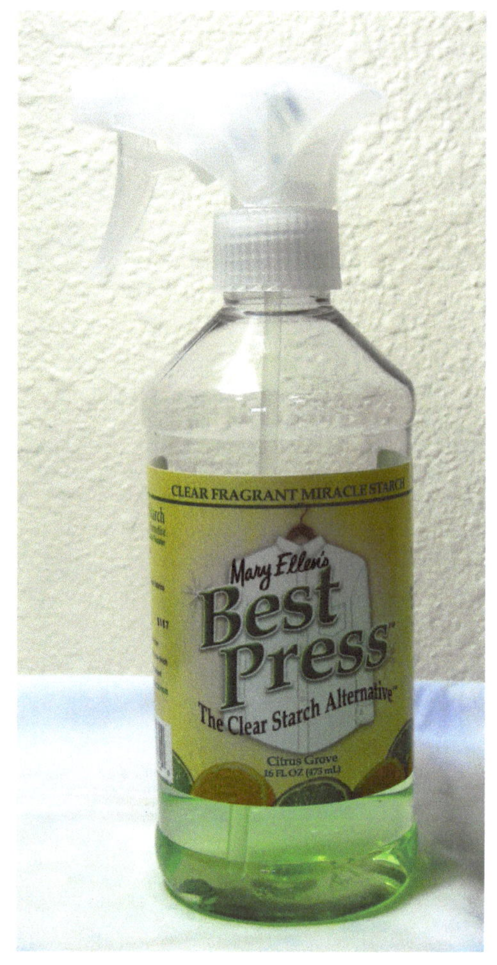

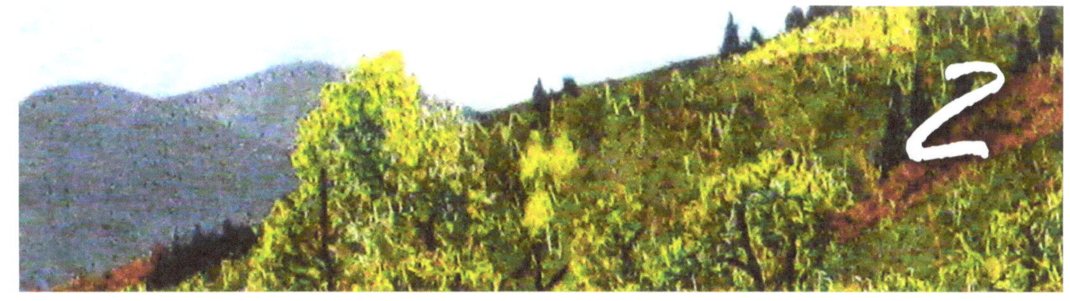

Selecting an Inspirational Photo

Finding the picture you want to make into a fiber painting is exciting. So pull out your old photo albums, go through the pictures you've saved on your computer and talk to your family and friends. Most of my inspirational photos were taken by family members or myself. You can also try searching for copyright-free photos on the internet. If you find a photo that you would like to use that someone else has taken, be sure to ask for their written permission before you use it.

When deciding on a photo, I look for distinct fore, middle and background interests. By interests, I mean areas that you will want to add embellishment to, or added stitching. If there is interest in each area, it will be easier to make your art piece look realistic and have dimension.

For your first project, I recommend finding a photo without any kind of reflection in a lake or stream. I will go into that in Chapter 6.

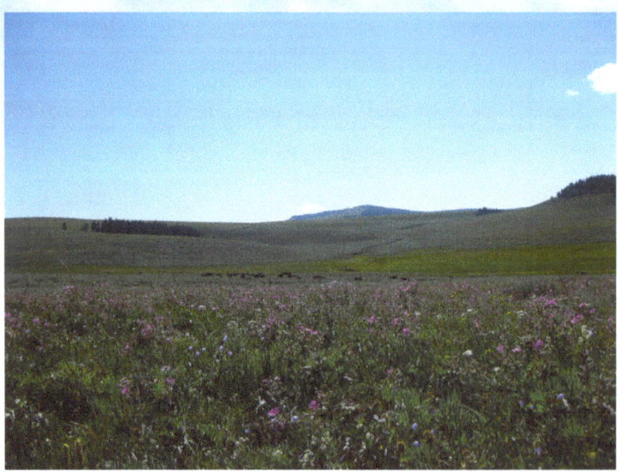

This picture doesn't have distinct areas. You would most likely add some stitching to the flowers in the foreground and a little for the trees in the background, but not much else.

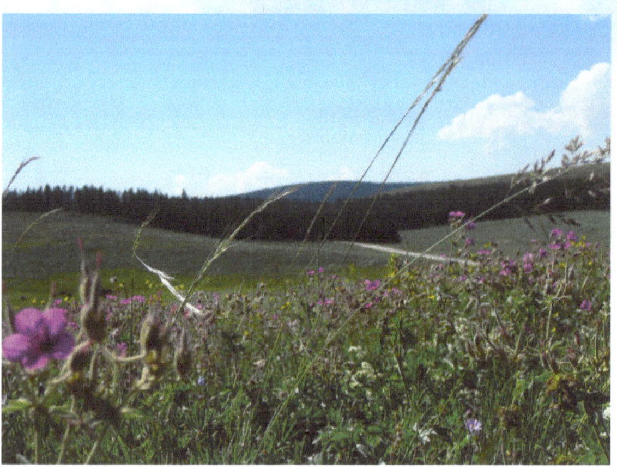

This picture has interest in the foreground, background and a little in the middle ground. Most of your added stitching would be on the flowers in front and the trees in the back. This picture would be better than the first.

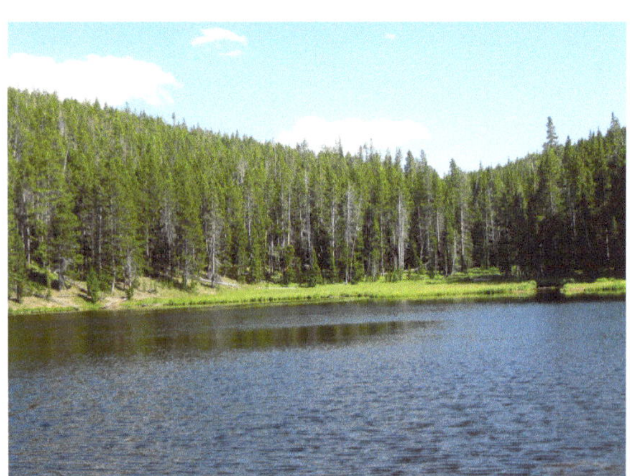

This picture doesn't have much interest, and it lacks "action." If there were some ducks or a person in a boat in the foreground, that would add some interest and color.

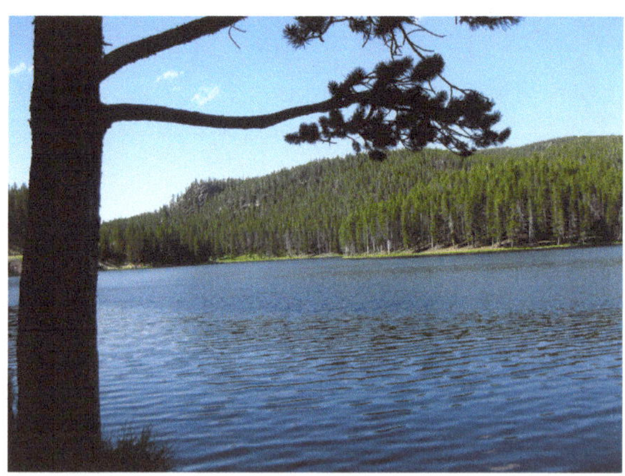

This picture has more interest because of the tree in the foreground. But I'd keep looking for another photo. This one is missing something of interest or "action."

If there is no interest in a certain section of the picture, it tends to make the fiber painting look "flat," or as though it lacks depth. That is because the fabric you use for that section will have little or no embellishing to make it come alive.

You may also find a picture that you like but has too much going on or too many details. Try cropping the picture to find an area with about equal interest in each section.

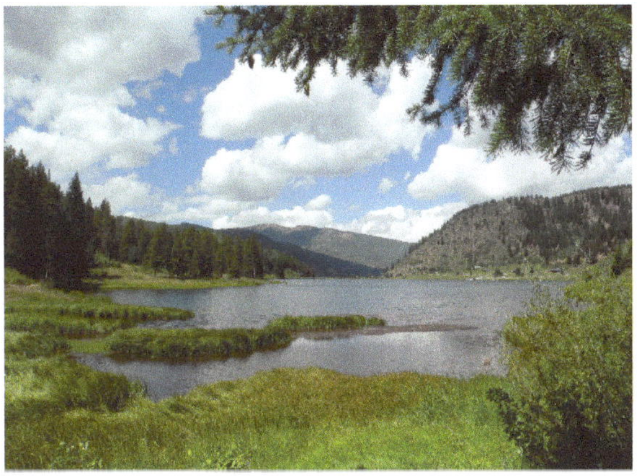

This picture has a lot of detail in the grasses near the water, and the trees both in the foreground and in the middle ground.

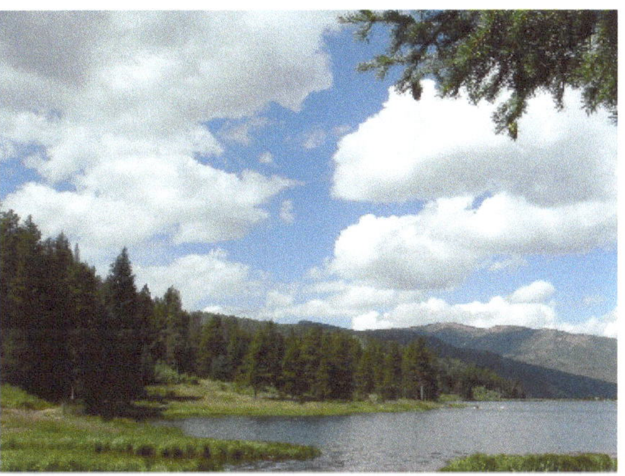

This cropped picture is nice, but is missing the bush in the front that added interest.

Once you have selected the picture you would like to use as your inspiration, enlarge or reduce it to an 8 ½" by 11" paper with a copy machine. This is a great size to start with. It will be easy to mat and frame later and won't be too overwhelming to start with.

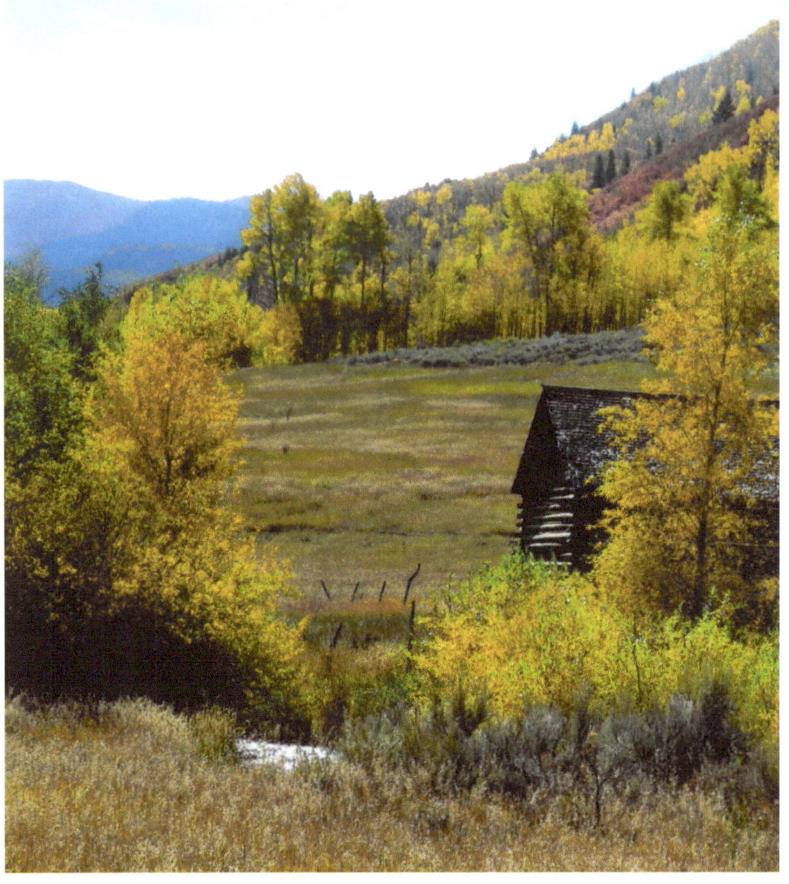

This is the picture I have chosen to use as my inspiration. It is a picture that was taken in Colorado by Amy Giertz. It has the fore, middle and background we're looking for. The hazy mountains and the big hill with the colorful trees and bushes are the background. The sagebrush and trees are the middle ground, and the cabin, grass, trees, and bushes up front will get lots of detailing. The fast-moving creek is the "action" we're looking for.

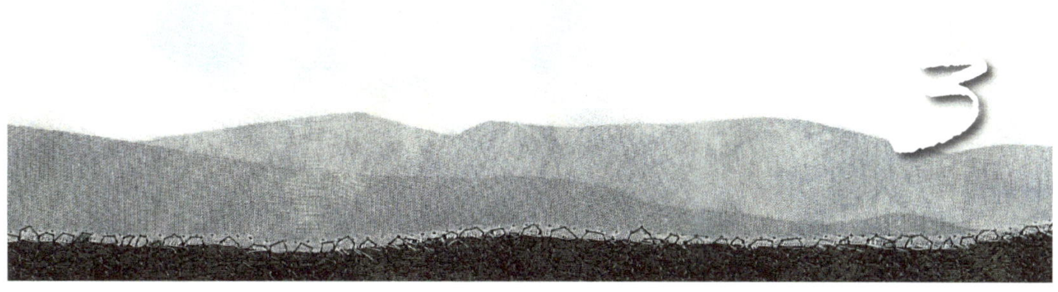

3

Preparing your "Canvas"

Prepare your "canvas" by using a light colored, cotton fabric, such as muslin, and applying a slightly smaller piece of fusible interfacing to the front of it. I like to use Pellon 808 Craft Fuse. It's an iron-on interfacing that gives the canvas some stiffness. The muslin should be approximately 12" x 15", or slightly larger than the outside measurements of the mat board.

Center a precut mat board over your canvas. Lightly mark the corners of the mat board opening with a pencil. Using those marks and a clear ruler, lightly draw lines that are ½" outside of them. This is the area you will be working in.

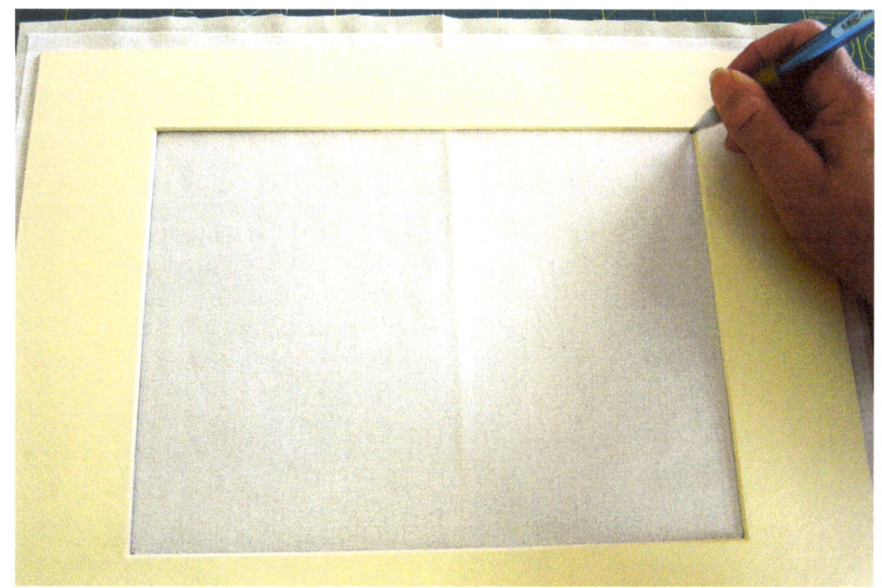

TIP

Have a couple of cream colored standard size mat boards on hand. They'll come in handy later as you'll see.

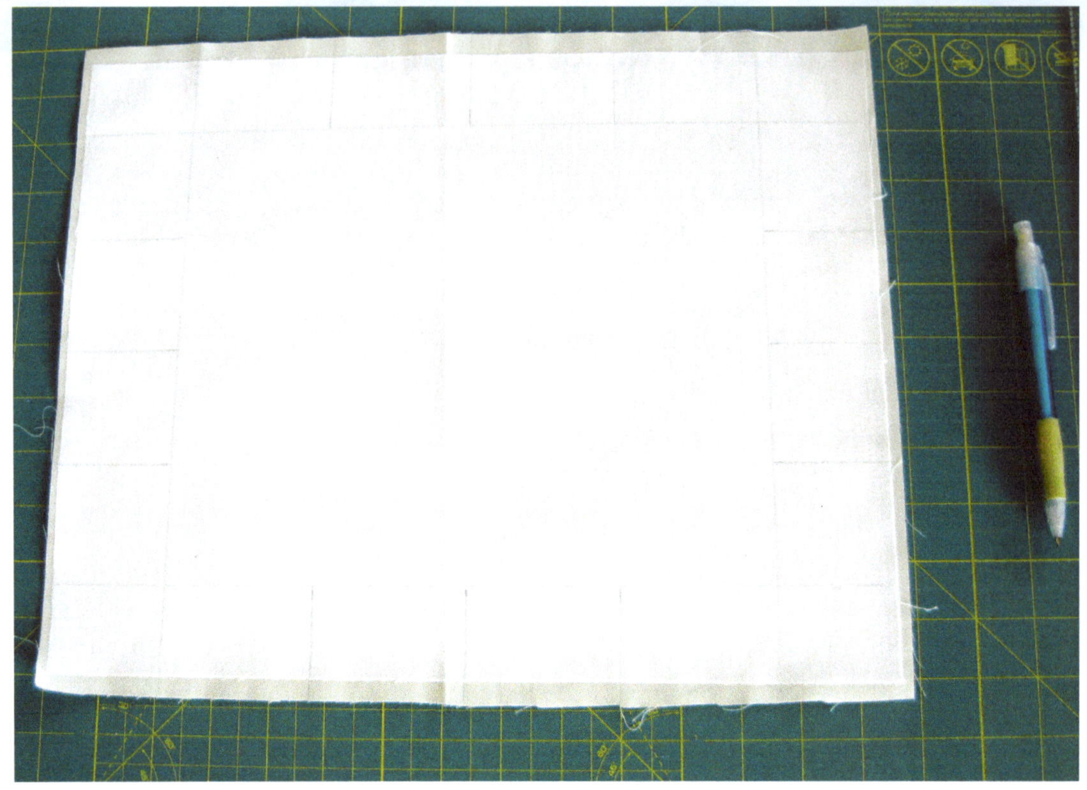

Along the outside perimeter lines you just lightly drew, divide each line into quarters. Lightly draw lines going out to the edges of your canvas. These will be your guidelines when working between your inspirational photo and your canvas.

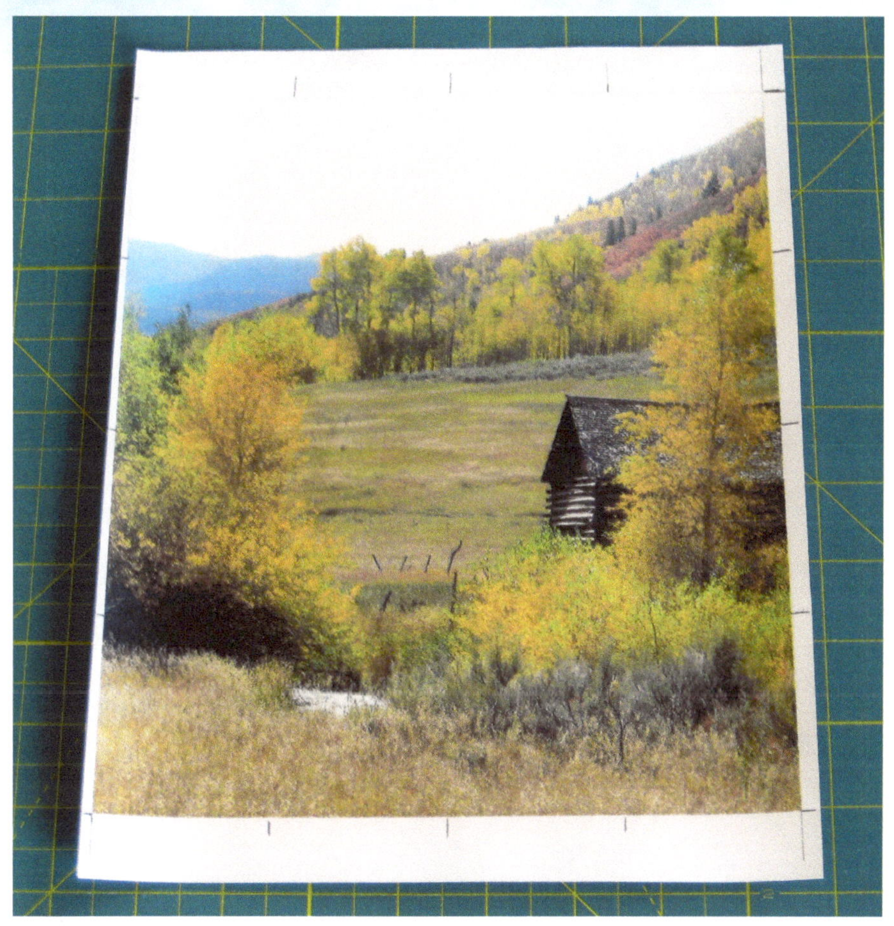

Take your photocopied picture and make marks along each of the sides in quarter increments.

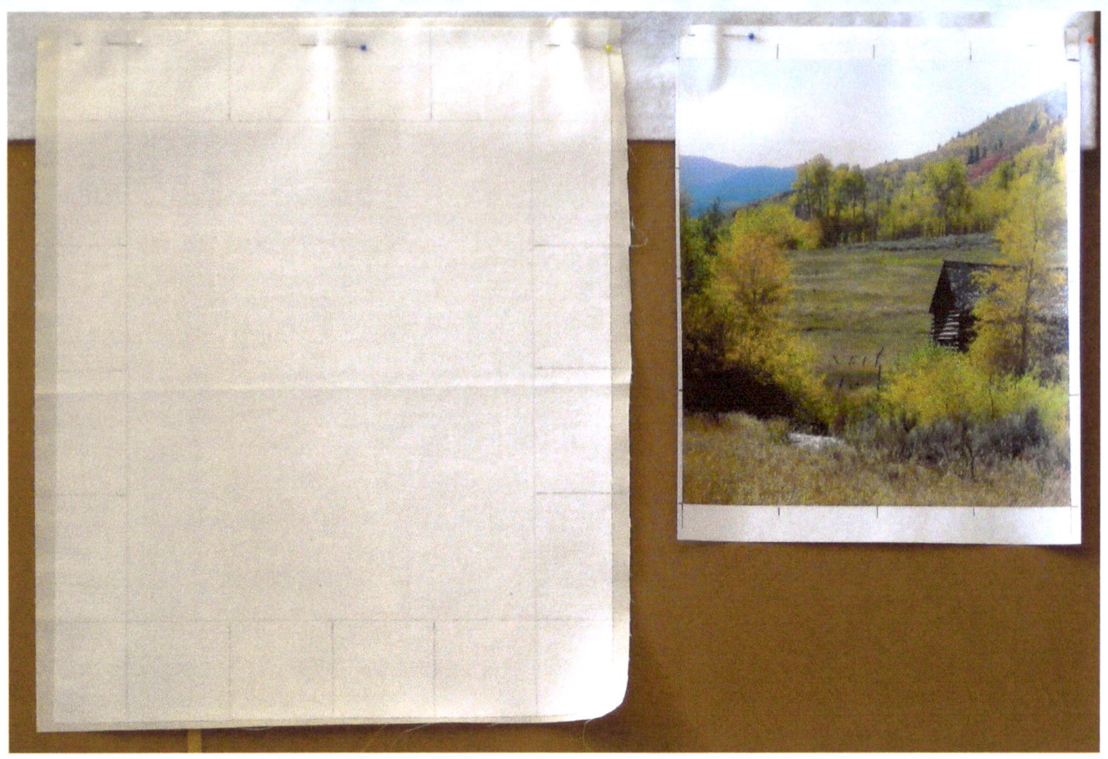

Hang your canvas with your inspirational photo copy on your design wall or easel board. Depending on where I'm working, I use both an easel and design wall.

I made my design wall using a 4' x 8' sheet of insulation board. First I covered it with a layer of polyester batting, and then topped that with a layer of white felt. Lighter weight fabrics will stick to the felt, and you can use pins for heavier pieces. I lean my design wall against a wall so I can move it around, but you can also screw it to the wall if you'd like.

TIP

I keep my fabrics in clear plastic tubs labeled by color.

My smaller easel is made of an artist's board. It's not fancy, but it's handy. I use a couple of large clips to hold a piece of batting across the handle side of the board. From that I can pin my canvas and picture. The easel's smaller sized board is nice if you're tight on space, or need to be able to move it around.

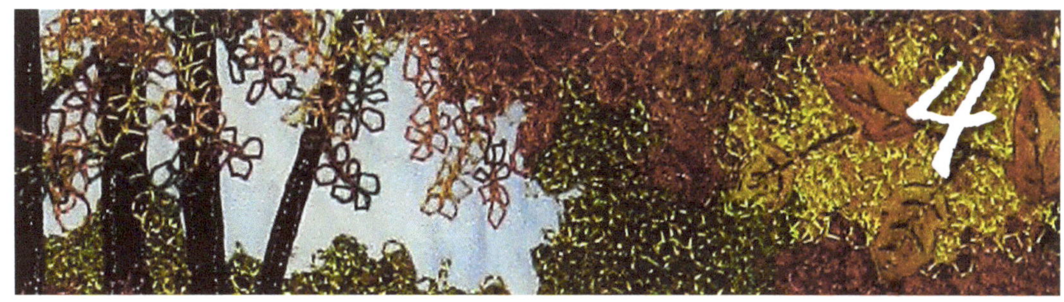

Getting Started and Selecting your Fabrics

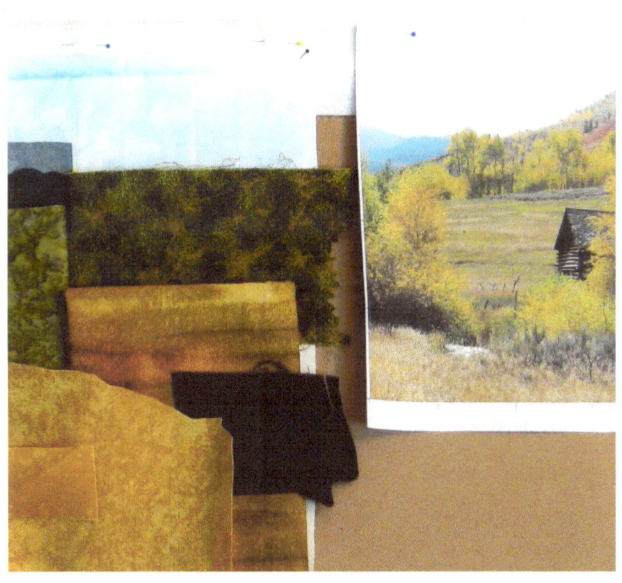

Sampling different fabrics

Now go through your fabrics and find ones that are as close in color to your photo as possible. If the fabrics are lightly printed, that is usually fine because you will be stitching over them when you add your embellishments. Don't forget to check the backsides of your fabrics. Sometimes that lighter shade is just what you need. Your embellishing can also lighten or darken the colors of the fabric a bit just by your choice of thread. You won't need fabrics for all the little details, just the most distinct and/or largest features in your photo. Either drape these fabrics over or pin them to your canvas. Stand back and see how the colors work together. Keep working with different fabrics until the colors feel right.

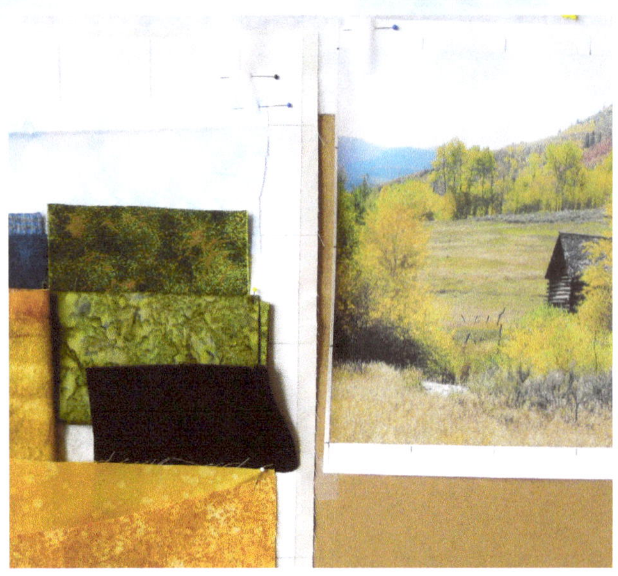

These are the fabrics I plan to use.

Now, using the marks you made on your photo and canvas as guidelines, cut pieces of the fabrics you want to use, cutting them slightly bigger than what you'll need. For example, the sky fabric will need to be about a quarter of the length of the canvas. The large hill is approximately half the length of the canvas, and the field fabric covers over half the length of the canvas.

Don't worry about cutting the shapes of the features yet. The bluish fabric I'm using for the mountains is actually a single fabric. I'm just using the wrong side for the mountain farthest back in the picture.

TIP

I like to use Mary Ellen's Best Press starch. It doesn't leave white flakes, and it smells really nice.

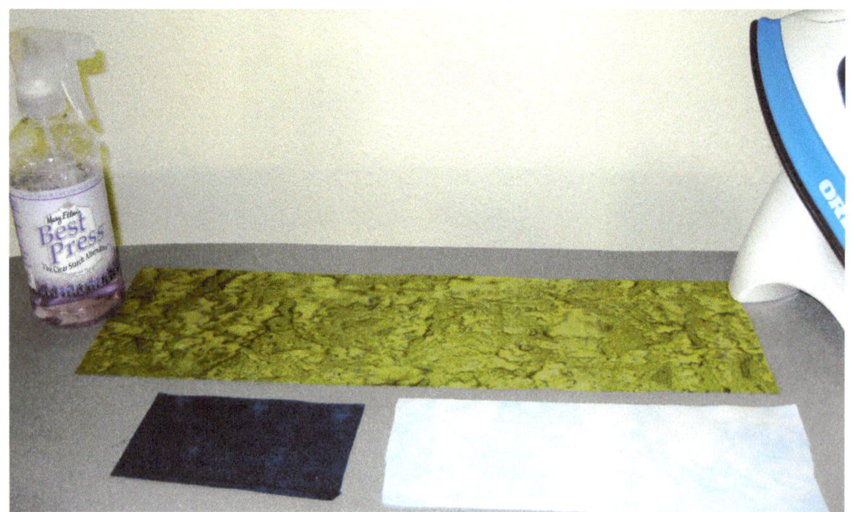

Iron all the pieces of fabric, then starch each piece about 3 times. You want the fabric to be slightly stiff. This is so that when you cut out your shapes and sew them onto your canvas, the fabric won't fray as easily. Also, the tighter the weave of the fabric, the less it will fray.

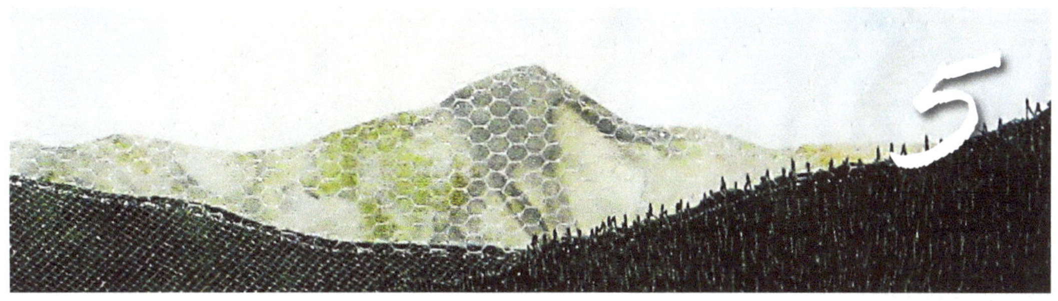

Applying your Fabrics to your Canvas

Start with the fabric you will be using for the farthest of your background features. Cut it so that the fabrics in the next layer will cover the raw edges. For my picture, the sky fabric is the farthest in the background. I will cut the fabric piece so that it covers the top part of the rectangle on my canvas. Making sure the piece is big enough that my next fabric pieces (the mountains and large hill) will cover the raw edge along the bottom of the sky. Using my adhesive spray, I stick the sky to my canvas. Now you will start to layer your fabrics from the background to the foreground with foreground pieces forming the top layer.

TIP

For small pieces of fabrics, you can use a glue-stick to stick them into place.

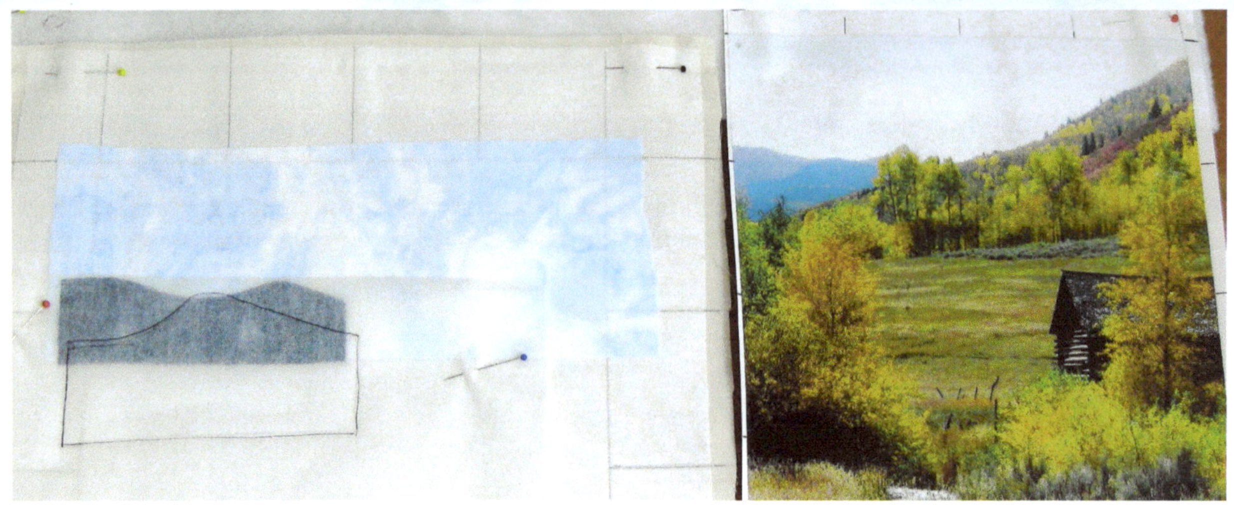

Using a piece of tracing paper pinned over your canvas, draw the next feature (mountains) onto the paper, using your inspirational photo copy as your guide.

In this picture I have already placed the fabric for the farthest mountain on my canvas, and now I am working my way forward and making a tracing paper pattern for the next closest mountain in the background. I will continue using this method until all of my basic fabric features are in place.

TIP

Remember that your canvas is slightly larger than your photo. So make your fabric pieces accordingly, using the outside guideline for reference. Once all of your stitching is done, the actual picture will be smaller, and closer in size to the photo.

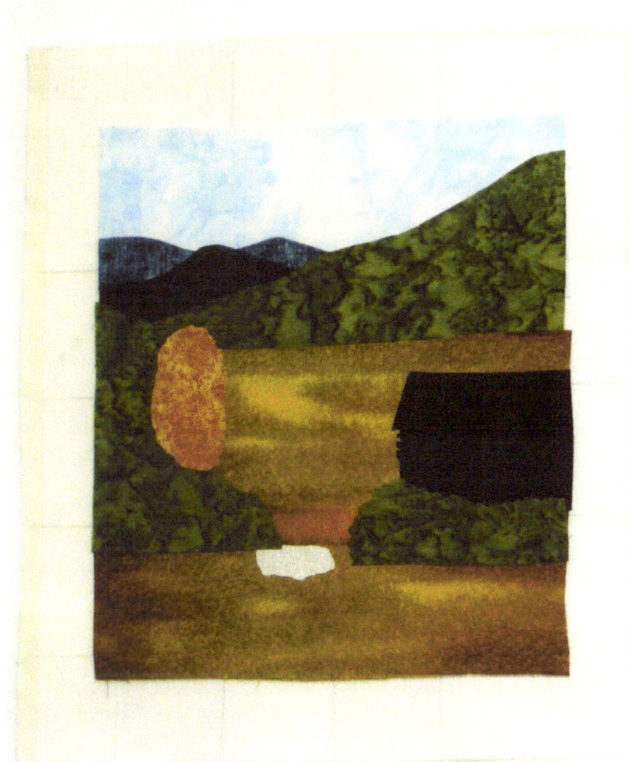

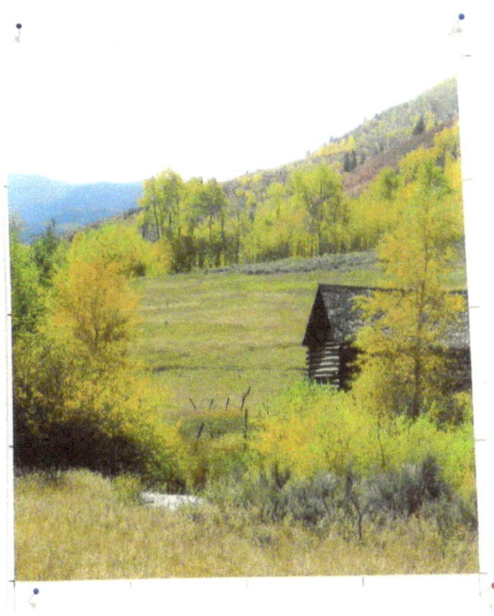

Notice that I didn't put yellow fabric over the cabin for the tree. I plan to make the tree just by using thread while I'm embellishing my picture later.

Any time I start sewing a new picture, I will change my sewing machine needle. I use a Universal 80/12 size needle. Use a needle that works well with several different types of threads. Also, put the feed-dogs down on your machine and use a darning foot. Practice sewing on some scraps of fabric to get the hang of moving the fabric while sewing.

Now that you have all your basic fabrics on your canvas, using invisible thread, stitch all the fabrics onto your canvas, stitching close to all the raw edges. I start by stitching the field fabric in place because it is centrally located. Then, I work my way out to the edges. This will make the canvas lay flatter. At this point, your canvas is beginning to look like your inspirational photo.

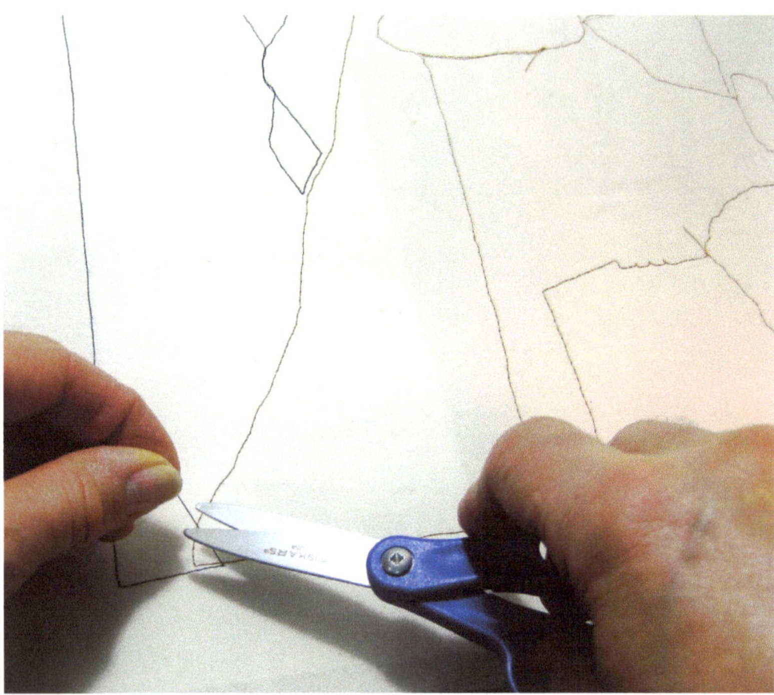

TIP

I don't use invisible thread in the bobbin. I use a neutral colored thread. It saves me adjusting the bobbin case tension.

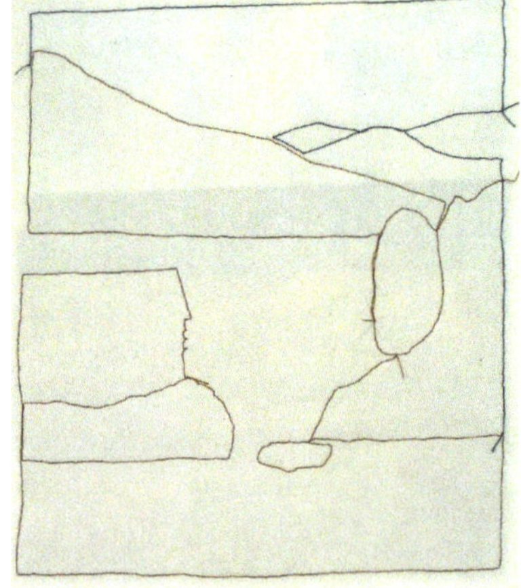

To make your finished picture tidy, with less thread ends sticking out, I pull all top threads to the back and hand-tie knots. To do this, when you cut your threads, leave about a 3" tail. Then put your picture face down and gently pull the bobbin thread up. This will pull a loop from the top thread to the back of your picture. Using the tip of a seam ripper or a pin, carefully pull that thread to the back without cutting it. Tie the two threads in a knot close to the fabric, and clip the threads to about ½". This is time consuming, but it keeps your picture neater.

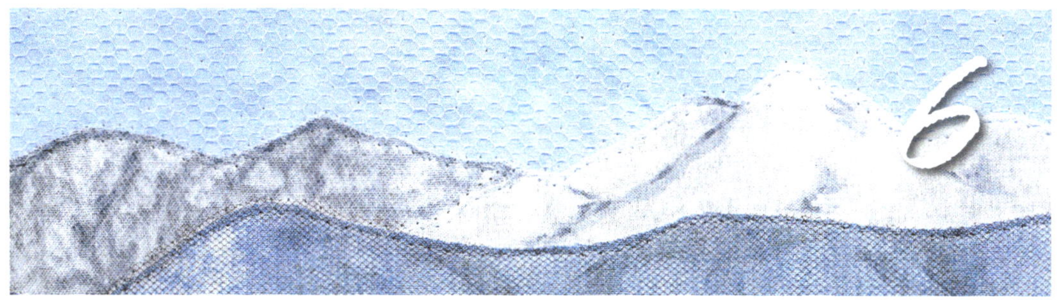

Stitching Techniques

I usually use the straight stitch and the zigzag stitch for my pictures. You will be using a free-motion type of sewing. Please refer to your sewing machine book for instructions regarding your particular machine.

Straight Stitches

Set your machine for a straight stitch, keeping the darning foot on and the feed dogs down. Use this stitch when stitching the fabrics to your canvas, and for creating close-up grasses, lines on structures, fence posts, tree trunks and branches, etc. You can use this same stitch and make many small loops and circles to make leaves on close-up trees and bushes as well.

Zigzag Stitches

Set your machine for zigzag stitches, keeping the darning foot on and the feed dogs down. I use this stitch a lot for trees, especially pine trees, and backgrounds.

For both the straight stitch and the zigzag stitch, you will move your canvas in either back and forth or circular motions, depending on the look you are after. Experiment with both stitches on a small practice canvas. Make a practice canvas the same way you would make a canvas for a picture; a layer of muslin, Pellon 808, and a top fabric. The top fabric can be anything you might have. Practicing on this will give you the feel of the thickness of the canvas, and for how to move your canvas around smoothly. Sometimes I find myself tensing up, but try to relax and have fun.

Sky

Most of the sky fabrics I use are hand-dyed. You can experiment by making your own, or purchase some. I usually buy mine from a quilting store. While hand dyed fabrics can be harder to locate, I try to avoid printed cloud fabrics. The machine printed patterns tend to be less realistic.

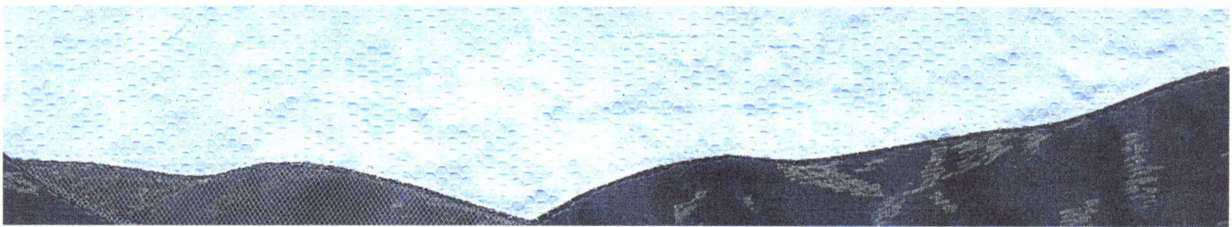

I found that I can make the sky look more textured if I put a layer of netting on it and then stitch a random swirly pattern, often called stippling, with invisible thread. Try not to cross your swirly stitches.

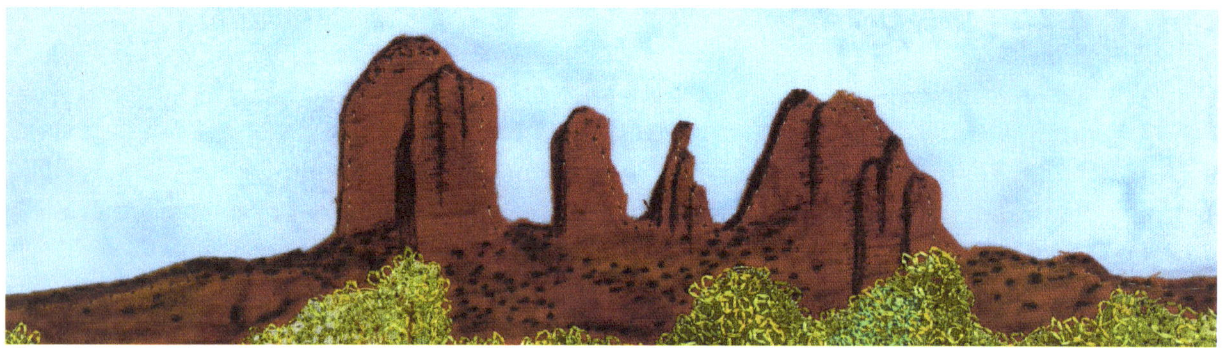

This sky doesn't have the netting on it. As a result, it has a flatter feel to it. However, I thought it made the picture feel more "hot and dry," like the desert.

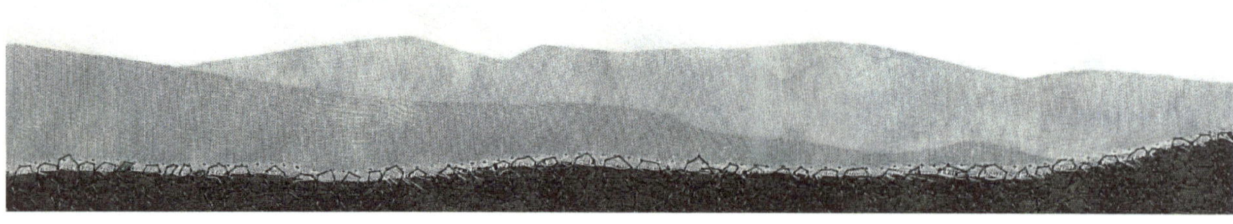

To make this sky look hazy, I used a layer of organza, as an overlay.

Water or Lakes

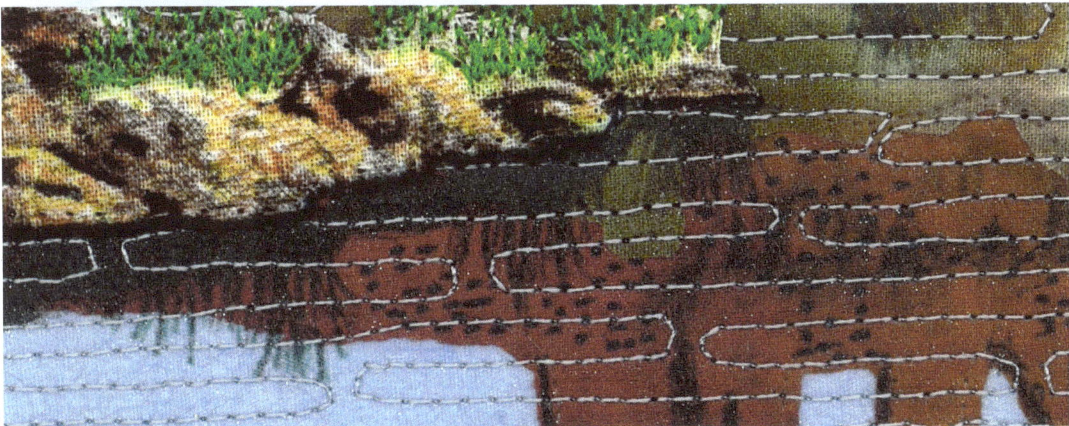

To make water look realistic, in most cases you'll want to add a reflection. In the picture above, you see the rock formations from the background and the shadows of the rocks and grasses from the foreground. For the grasses I used a straight stitch. For the waves in the water I also used a straight stitch and randomly went back and forth to create a watery look. When I was making this picture, I cut two identical pieces of fabric for the large rock formations in the background, cutting them with right sides together. Unfolding it makes the reflection in the water. I also did that with the tree fabric that you can't see too well in this picture. An example of this can be found in the gallery in chapter 9. Then I put a layer of gray sheer fabric over the reflection part of the image. Be sure to add detailing to the reflection fabric before you layer your sheer fabric on top.

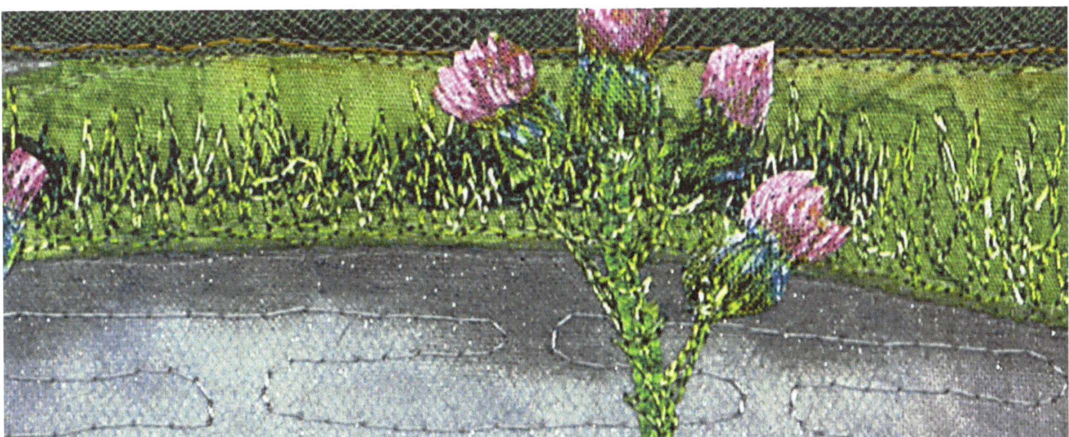

In this picture, the water is not so clear, so the reflections of the hills in the background appear more as shading rather than distinct features. Again I layered a sheer fabric over the reflection fabric, which was a piece of sky fabric, and used a straight stitch and randomly went back and forth. For that, I used a medium gray thread made out of rayon to give it a little sheen.

Mountains

When making mountains, make sure the colors get lighter as the mountains get farther away. This will give your picture more depth and realism.

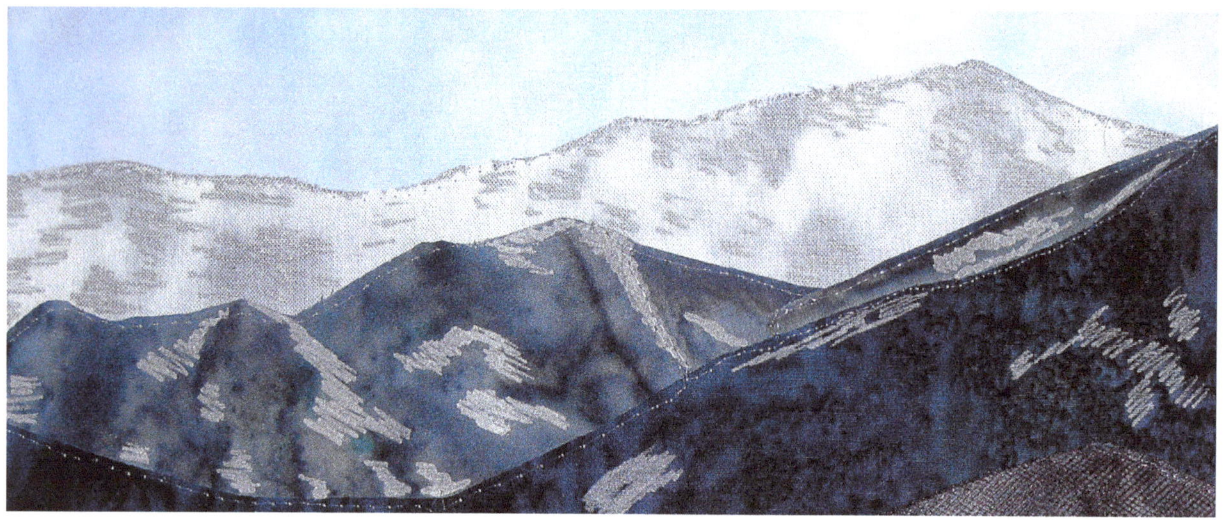

On the mountains above I used hand-dyed fabrics and permanent markers.

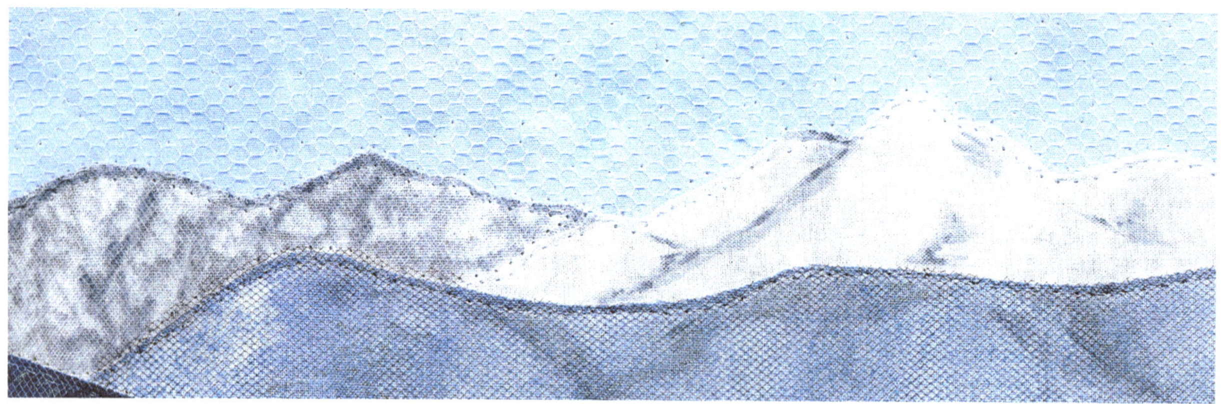

On these mountains, I used hand-dyed fabrics, markers, and some tulle.

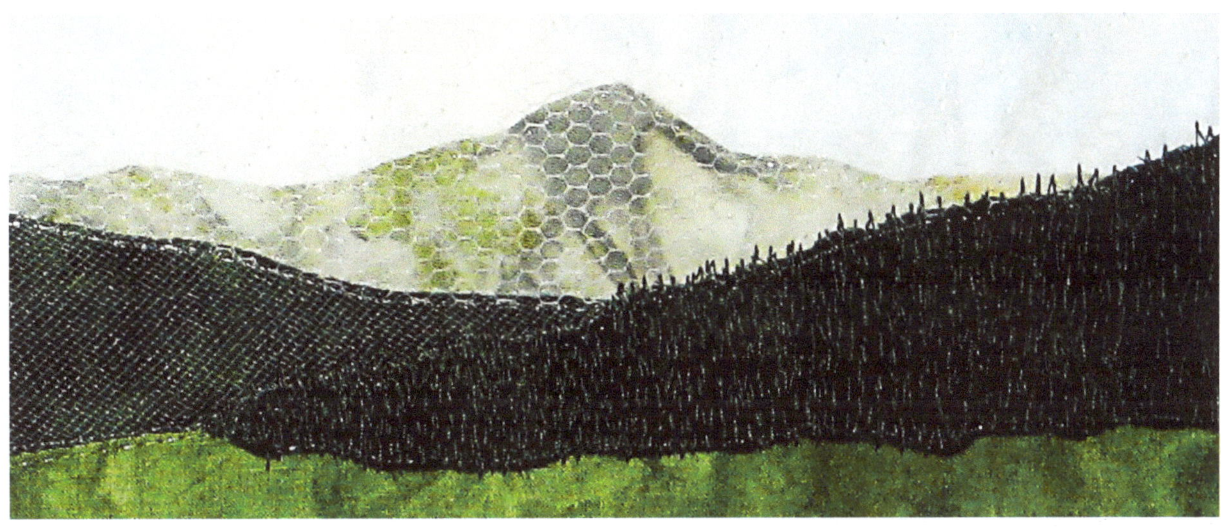

On these mountains I used hand-dyed fabrics. The farthest mountain and the sky have netting over them. The two green hills are actually the same fabric. The fabric for the hill farther away is the “wrong side” of the darker green hill. Then I covered it with tulle. The closest hill uses a zigzag stitch and dark green thread to make pine trees.

Trees

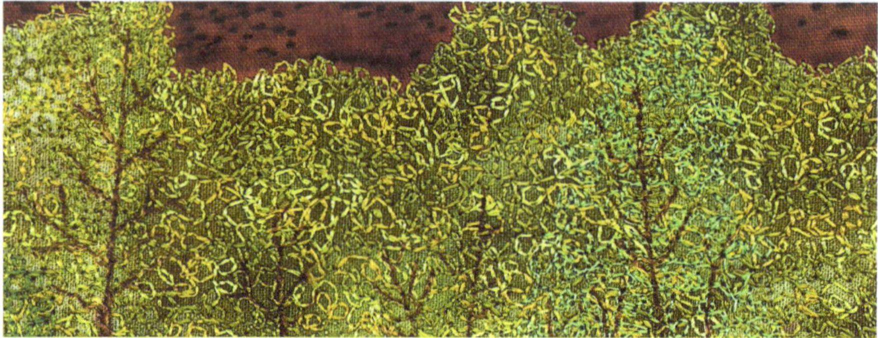

For the trees above, I used one piece of hand-dyed fabric. Then I used a straight stitch and made lots of little loops with a variegated thread to make the leaves. Next, I went in and drew the tree trunks with a permanent pen to define where I wanted each of the trees. Finally, I went back in and used yellow and green thread to define some of the trees. Sometimes I'll also stitch the tree trunks with a dark thread to make them stand out more.

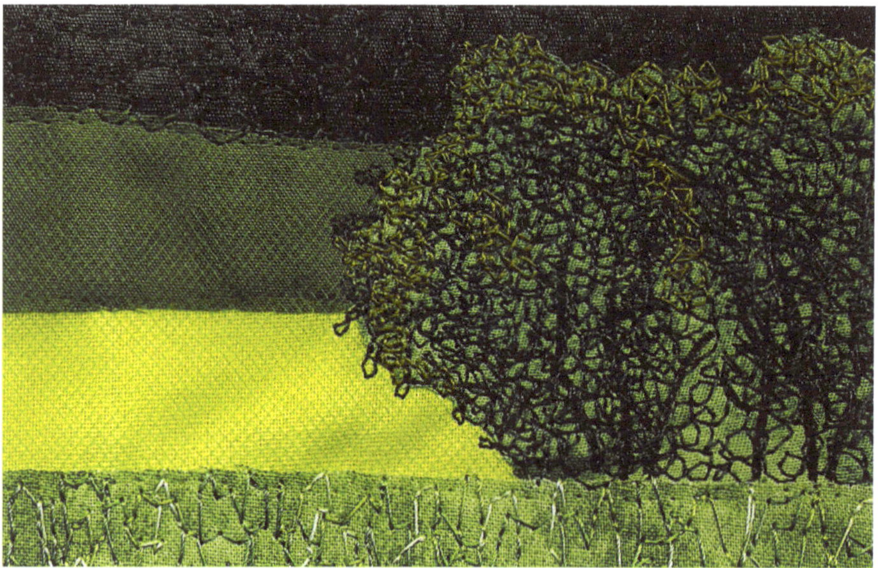

These trees are made again with only one piece of fabric, covered with lots of little loops. I made the loops using a straight stitch. Then, I drew the trunks in and added the lighter green thread to make the trees look more three-dimensional.

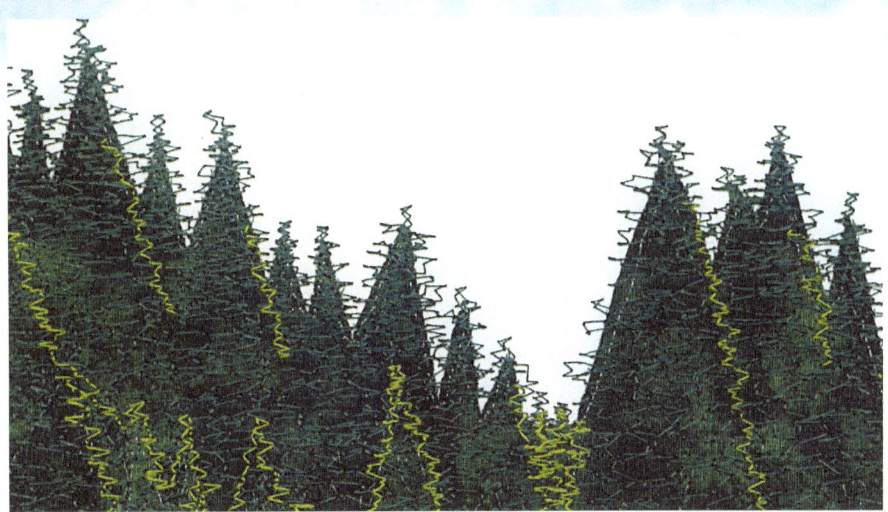

For these pine trees, notice how I went outside of the green fabric with my stitches. I used a random zigzag stitch to do that. I also defined some of the trees by using a lighter colored green thread.

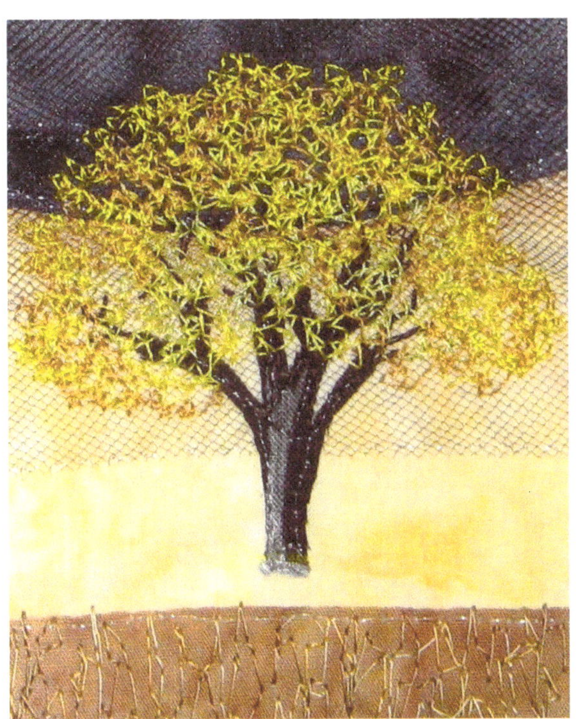

The leaves in this tree are made by using only thread and no fabric. I used a random zigzag stitch and a variegated thread for these leaves. I added a bright yellow rayon thread to make the tree look as if the sun is shining on it. Rayon has some sheen to it, where a regular cotton thread does not.

Animals

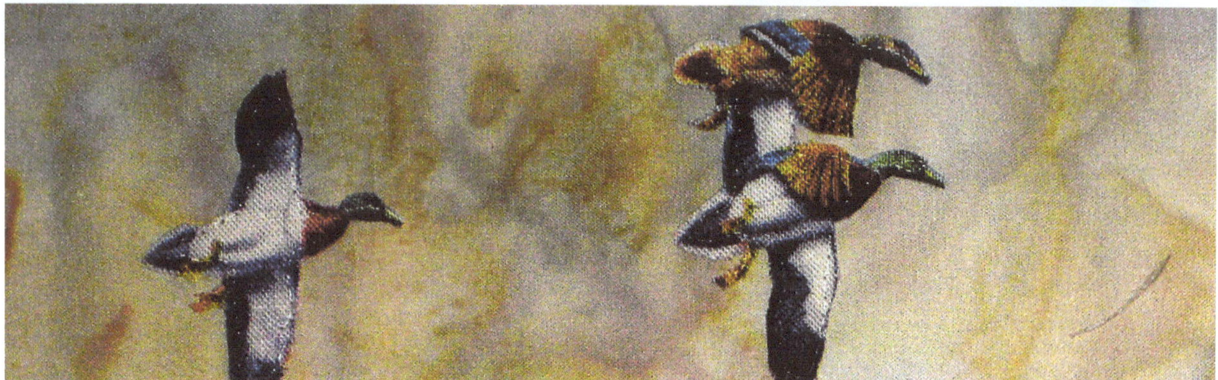

It's sometimes hard to find realistic animals on cloth from the fabric store. Oftentimes, they aren't posed correctly for the image I'm creating. For example, horses are often depicted as running, but I want them to be grazing. Or I want an animal and I can only find part of it printed on a fabric with a bunch of other things. For the grazing horses I needed for a picture I was working on, I actually went out and found some grazing horses, took a picture of them and then printed it on fabric using my printer. You can find printer fabric at most quilt and fabric stores. Use white fabric, because you want the colors to be as true as possible. After you have your animals on your picture, you can add some detailing by stitching areas to make them stand out, or use pens to touch them up.

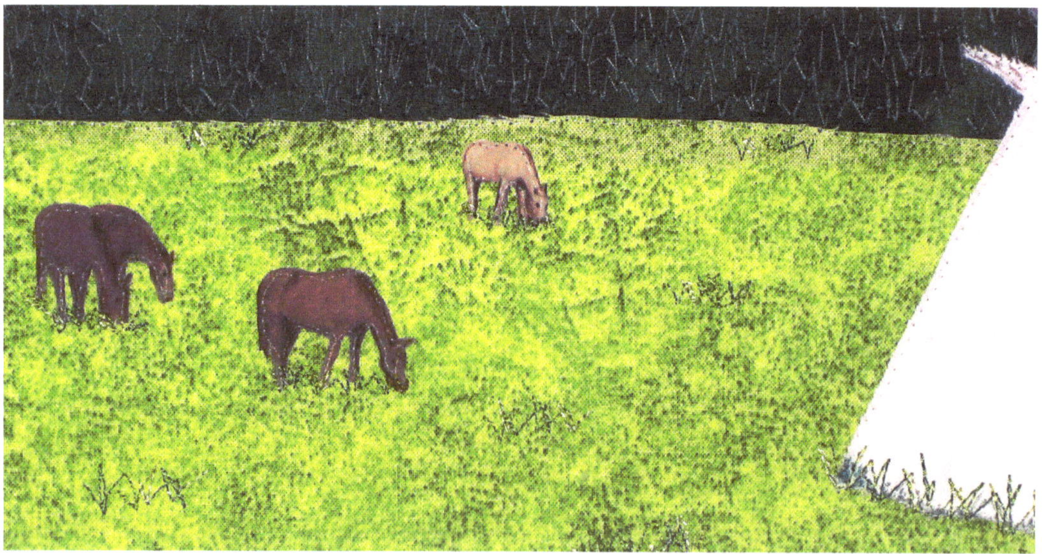

The horses in this picture are from a work in progress. They were from a picture I took and then printed on fabric and cut out and applied to this picture.

Streams

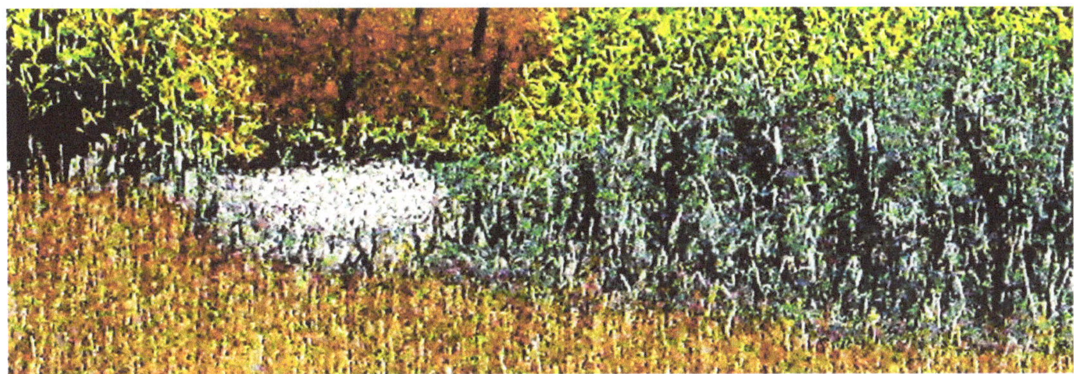

When making streams, I want the water to appear as if it is moving, or the sun is shining off of it. To create this effect, I quite often use a shiny rayon or metallic thread. In the picture above, I used a silver metallic thread. On the picture below, I used a shiny gray rayon thread to run stitches back and forth. On other pictures, I have also used a small sponge and white acrylic or fabric paint to dab a little color onto my picture.

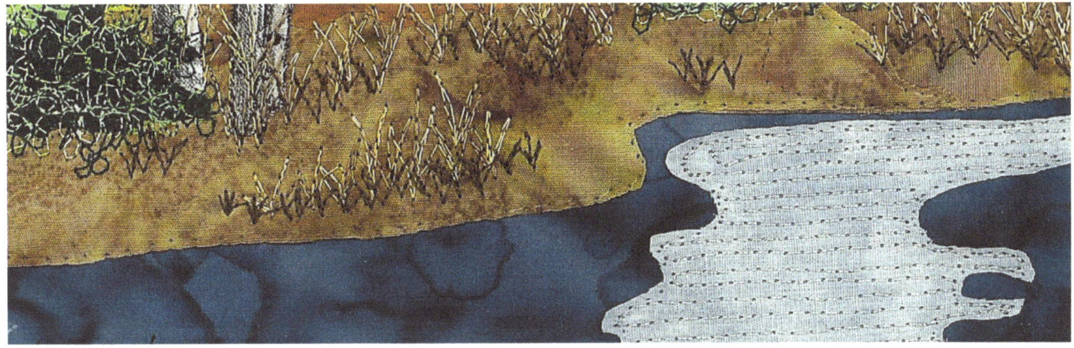

Embroidery

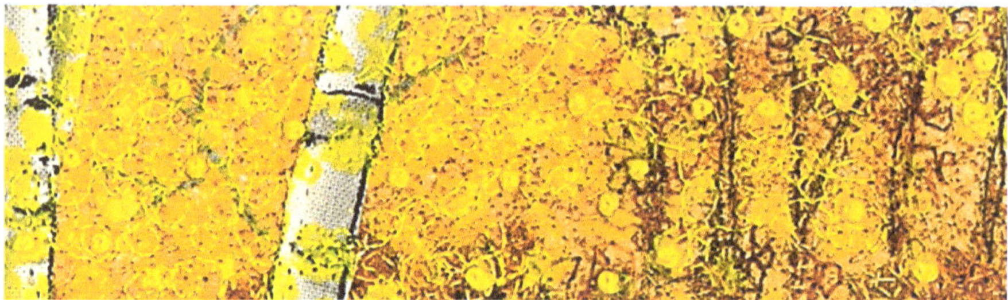

I use embroidery floss to add a third dimension to my pictures. On the picture above, I added lots of yellow French-knots to the yellow leaves to make them stand out. In the same picture I used some red floss to add leaves to the bushes at the bottom of the picture. For more examples, see "Birches" in the gallery of pictures in chapter 9.

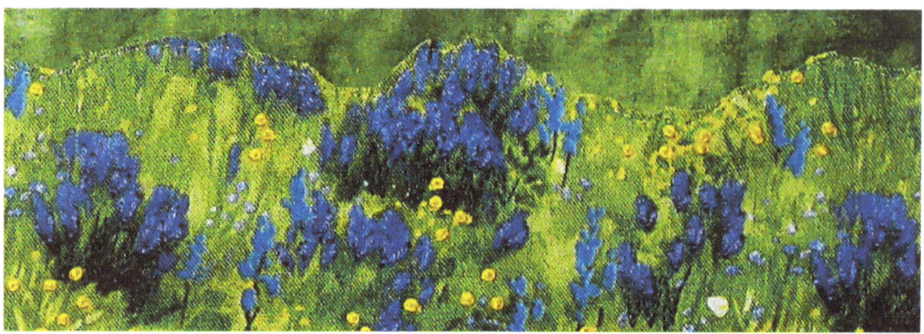

In the picture above, from "Big Horn Meadow," I made yellow French-knots for some of the flowers and then used some blue embroidery floss to accent the blue flowers.

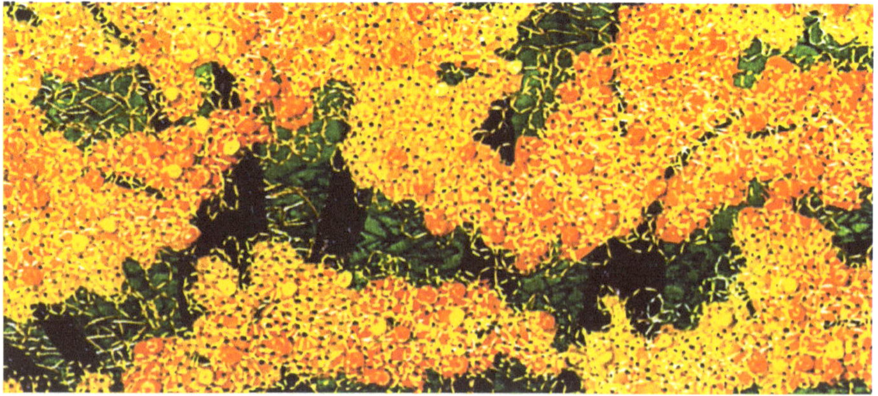

In the picture above, from "Quiet Backyard", I again used French-knots and made yellow, orange-yellow and orange 3-dimensional leaves.

For this picture, I cut some small leaves from a printed fabric and stitched down their centers to attach them to the picture. I then used a dark brown marker to draw the veins of the leaves in.

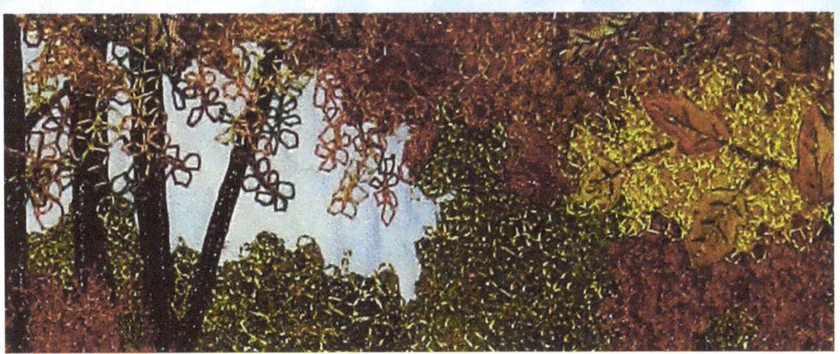

Acrylic and Fabric Paint

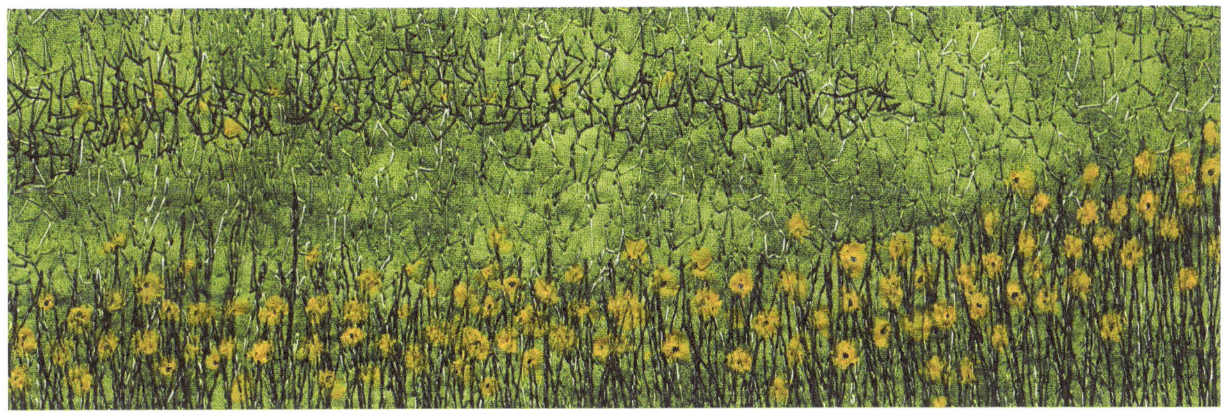

I have used acrylic and fabric paints to add features, and highlight features on different pictures. In the example above, I painted the yellow flowers using acrylic paint. Then I used a black marker to dot a few centers of the flowers. For the picture below I used white fabric paint to add some highlighting to the mountains in the background. I also did some stitching to make the valleys and ridges stand out more.

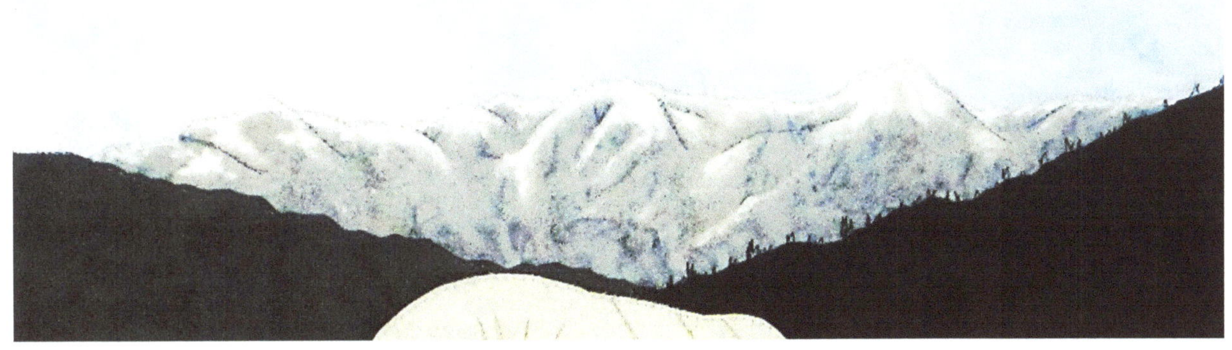

Pens

I use permanent markers quite a bit in my pictures. I use them to make things look more realistic and stand out, I fill in stitched areas, and I add shadows and accents.

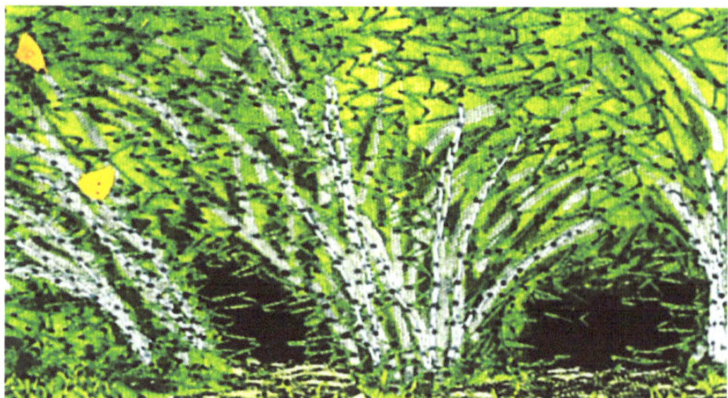

For the bushes above, I used a silver Sharpie to draw in the trunks. Then I went back in and used a straight stitch to highlight the trunks. Notice also that I used very small pieces of fabric to make the falling leaves in this picture (Quiet Backyard).

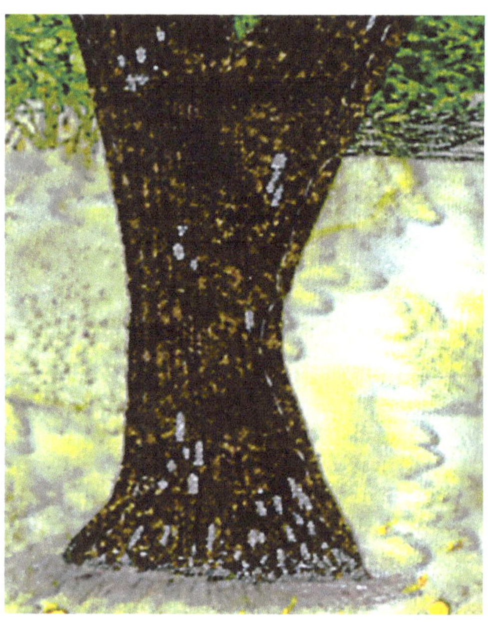

In the same picture, I used the silver Sharpie to draw the little highlights on the trunk of the tree.

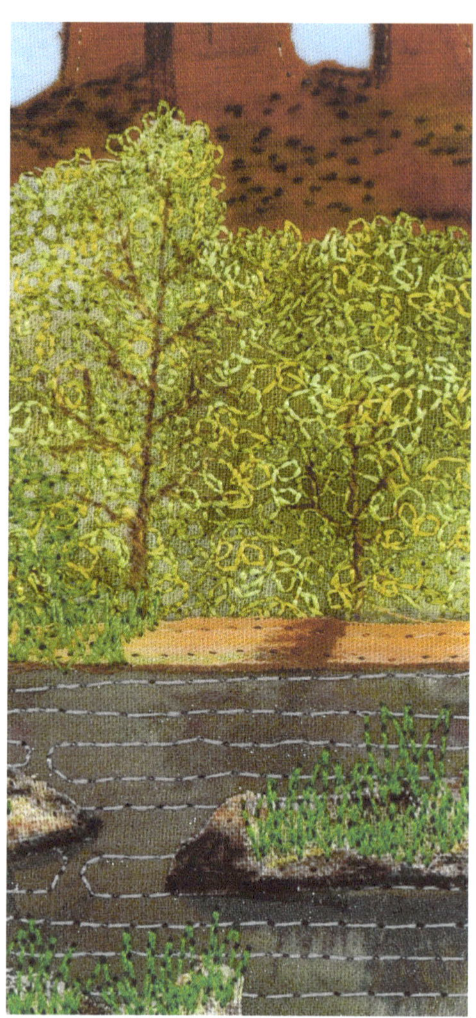

In this picture, "Arizona Afternoon," I drew the trunks of the trees in and then used a straight stitch to darken them a bit more. I also dotted the hills in the background to look like small bushes and vegetation.

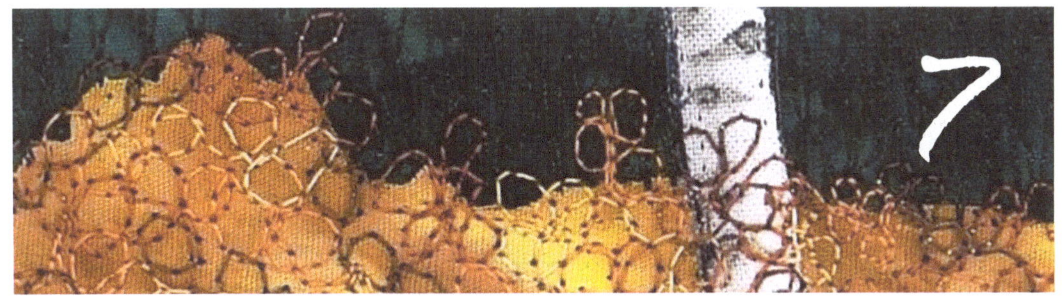

Making your Picture Come Alive

Now let's make our picture come alive.

You will want to add your embellishments in the order that you applied your fabrics to your canvas. That way, embellishments in your foreground will be over, or be on top of the background and the middle ground areas. This is what will give the picture depth. If you plan to stitch some embellishment over your sky, such as trees, embellish your sky now. If you won't be embellishing over your sky fabric, you should wait and embellish the sky last, especially if you plan to use netting; you don't want to damage the netting while embellishing the rest of the picture.

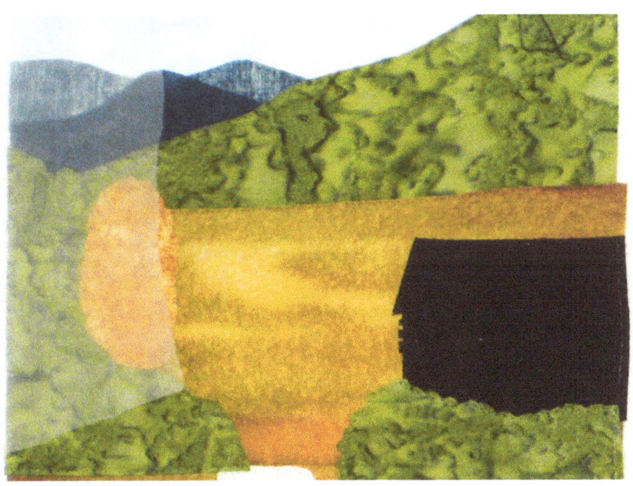

For my picture, I will start embellishing my mountains, because I may do some embellishing on the sky later. Sometimes your background layers don't have a lot of embellishing. That's okay.

The mountains in my photo look a little hazy. So I experimented by holding pieces of tulle and organza over the mountains to tone down the blue fabric a bit. I decided on two layers of organza. I used invisible thread to sew the organza into place, being careful while stitching along all the mountain fabric edges.

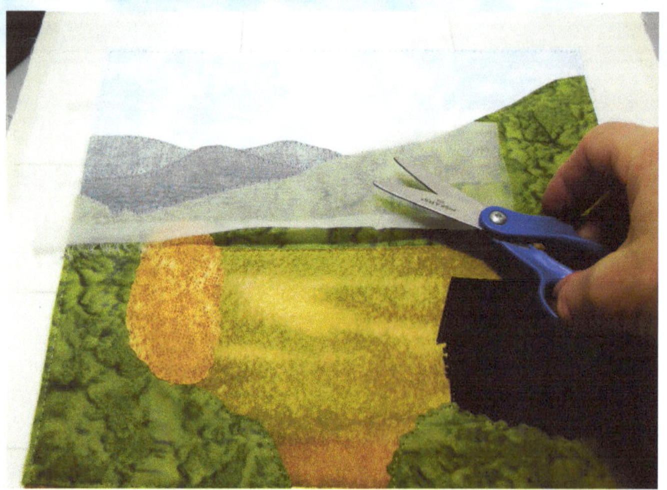

After sewing the organza into place, I carefully trim around the stitching with round-tipped scissors.

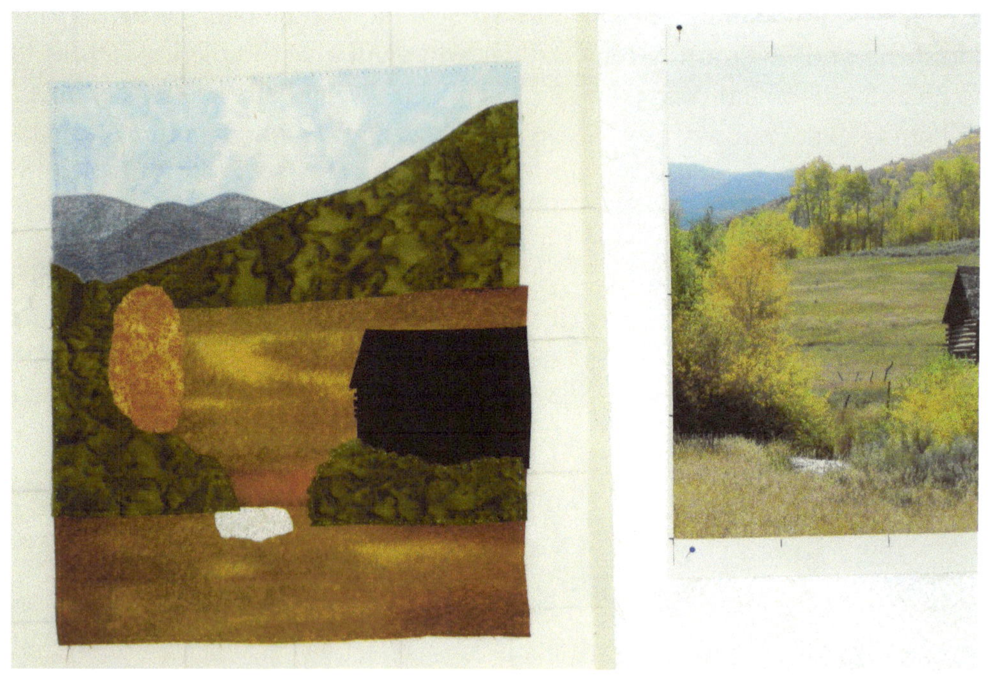

Now my mountains look hazy.

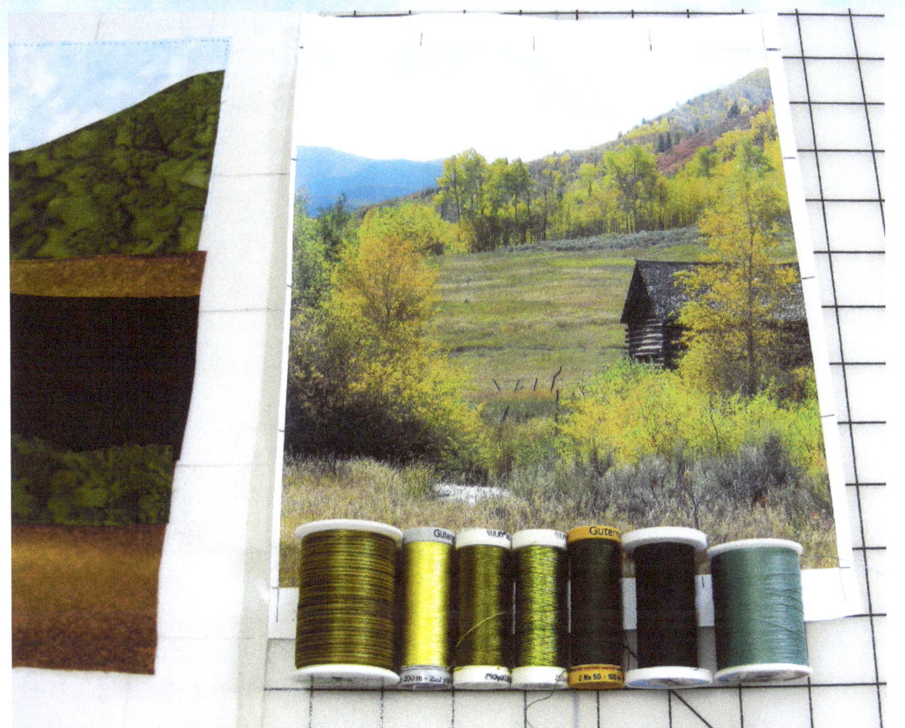

TIP

If you don't have the right colors of thread at home, take your inspirational photo to the store to pick them out. I use various brands, it's the color I'm after.

My next step will be the big hill with all the trees on it. I'm going to use a variegated thread as a "fill-in" for the overall trees on the hill. The picture above shows some of the threads I plan to use for my picture. It may change as I work on it, and there will probably be a lot more, but this is a starting point for the thread selection.

TIP

I quite often use a slightly different color thread in the bobbin. It makes it much easier to see the threads when you pull them through to tie.

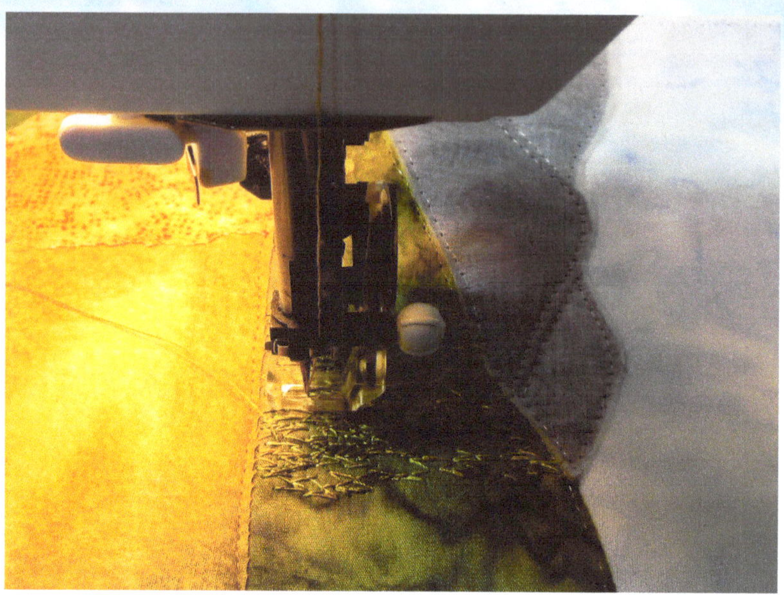

Here I am filling in the large hill with trees. To do this, I'm using a variegated thread, the zigzag stitch and a small circular motion. Notice that I have my picture perpendicular to the machine. I want the trees to look up and down and not sideways. I will fill in the whole area of the big hill with this variegated thread.

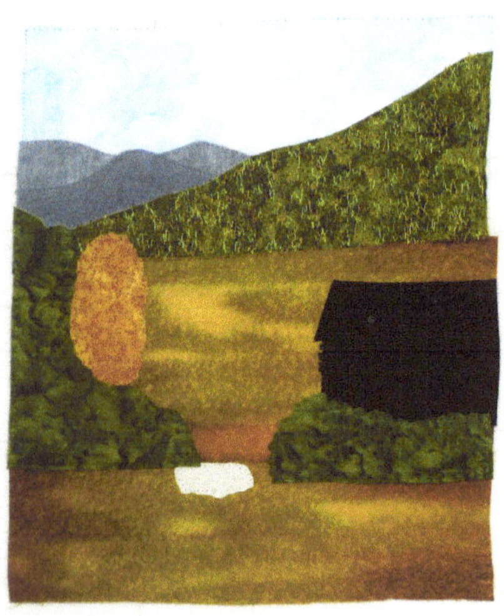

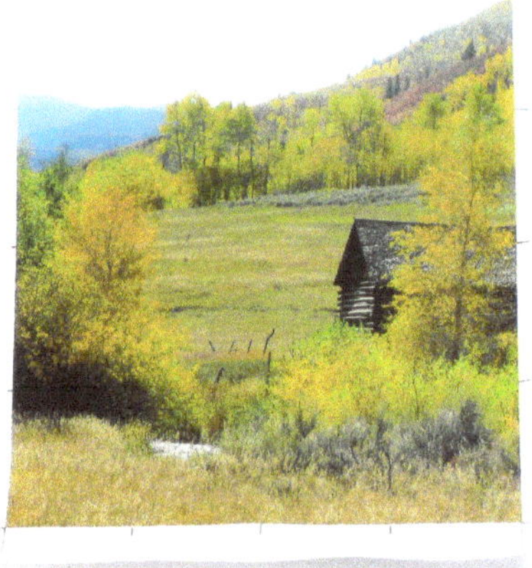

As you start doing the stitching on your picture, you will begin to notice more and more of the details. I now notice more of the brownish areas on the hill. I'll want to go in and fill that in. I'll do that with some variegated brown thread. Then I'll use some dark green and yellow thread to make the individual trees. Notice how the pine trees along the top of the hill overlap onto the sky fabric, and the hazy mountain. I'm again using the random zigzag stitch to make these trees.

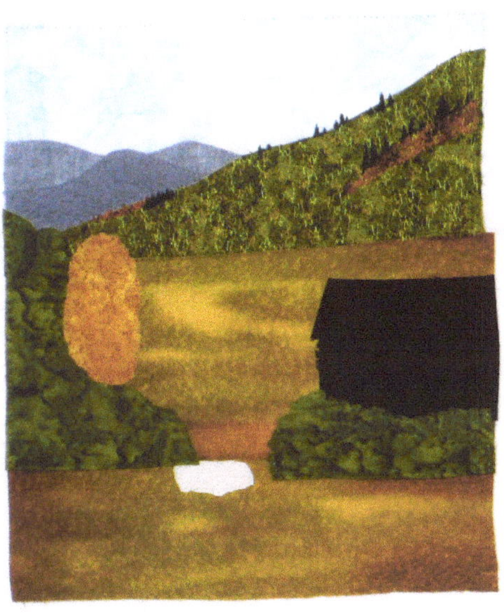

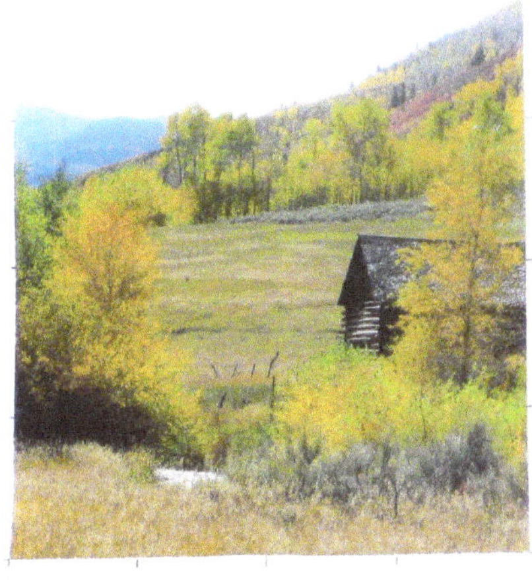

For the placement of the trees, I use the marks I made around the perimeter of the photo and the canvas as a guide.

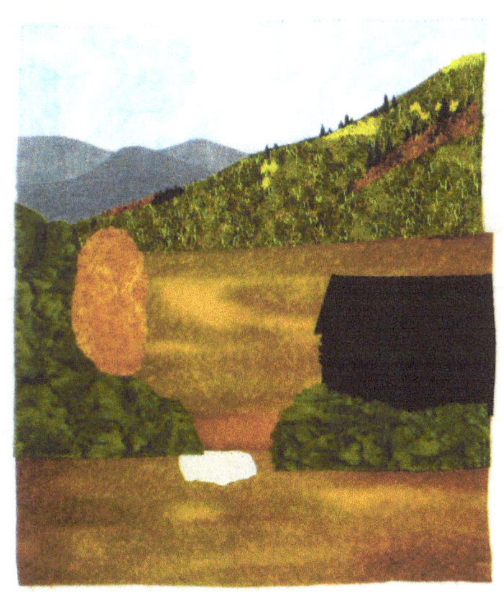

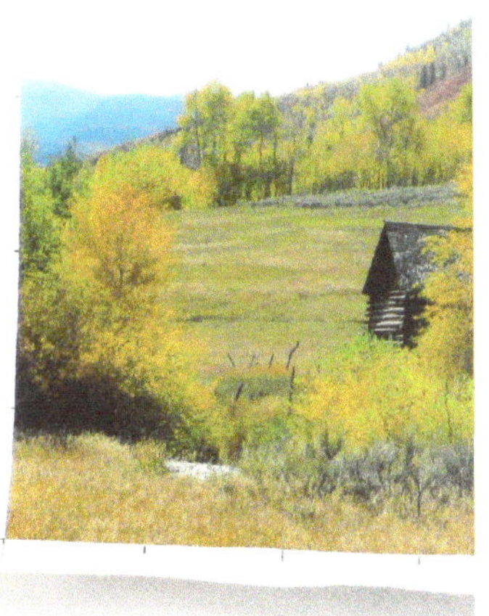

TIP

As you use your different colored threads, set them aside so that if you want to go back and fill in or add more color, you don't have to hunt for the color you had used.

Now I'll make the row of trees at the base of the hill. I'm going to continue using the zigzag stitch, but with smaller stitches and a lighter green variegated thread.

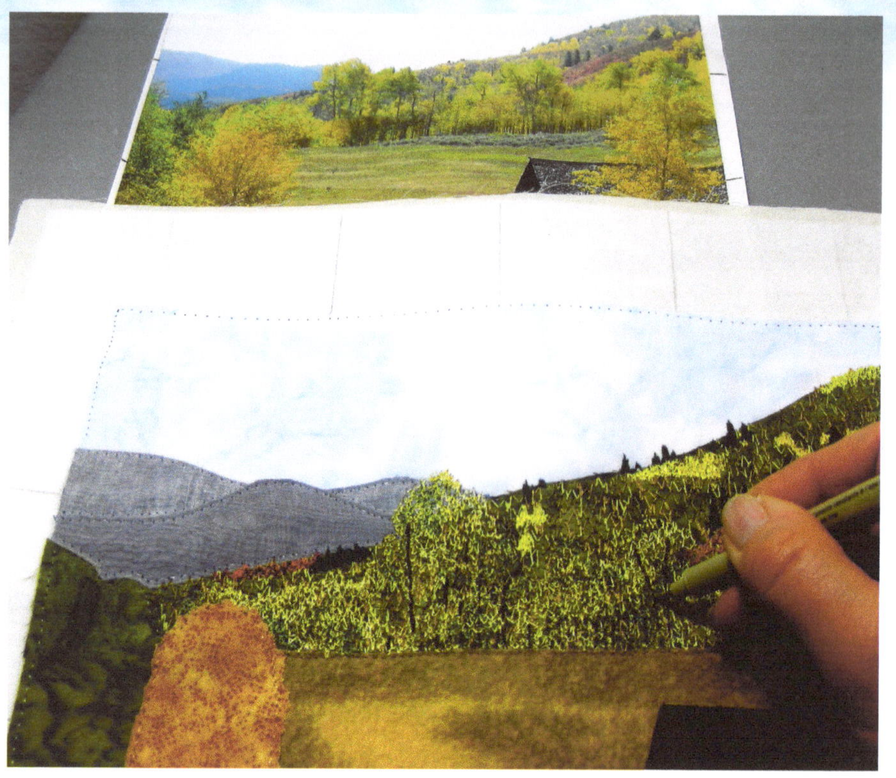

I'll use a dark brown permanent marker to draw the trunks of these trees in. After drawing the tree trunks I get a better idea of where I need to go in and add some bright yellow and green highlights on the trees. Again, I continue to use the zigzag stitch, moving the canvas around randomly to get the look I want. Remember it doesn't have to be perfect or exactly like the photo. You're using the photo as your inspiration. Just have fun with it.

Notice that I did go back and use a straight stitch and dark brown thread to emphasize some of the tree trunks along the base of the hill.

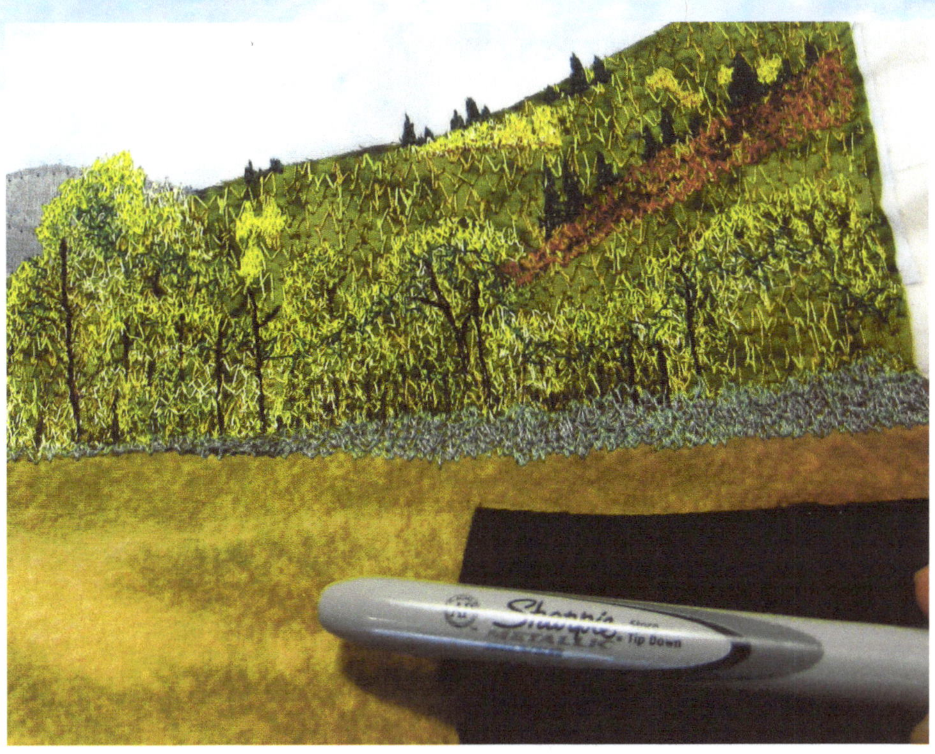

Now I'm going to put the sagebrush in front of that row of trees. I continue to use the zigzag stitch. Some of the fabric behind the bushes shows, so I'm using a silver Sharpie to cover it up. The silver pen looks like a light gray, which blends well with the sagebrush. I then go back, and using a black fine tip permanent maker, I shade the bushes. Now they look more three-dimensional.

TIP

Test markers on scraps of the same colored fabric to see if it's the color you're wanting before marking on your picture.

TIP

Every once in a while, put your picture and photo on your design wall and step back and look at it. How's it looking? Do you need to go in and add anything to what you've already done?

Because I'm not quite sure what I want to do in the field area, I am going to work on the trees on the left side of the picture. First I'm going to use a dark thread and fill in the dark shadow, at the base of the trees on the left, again using the zigzag stitch and a black permanent marker. I'm doing this first because I'll want to put some leaves and grass over the shadow.

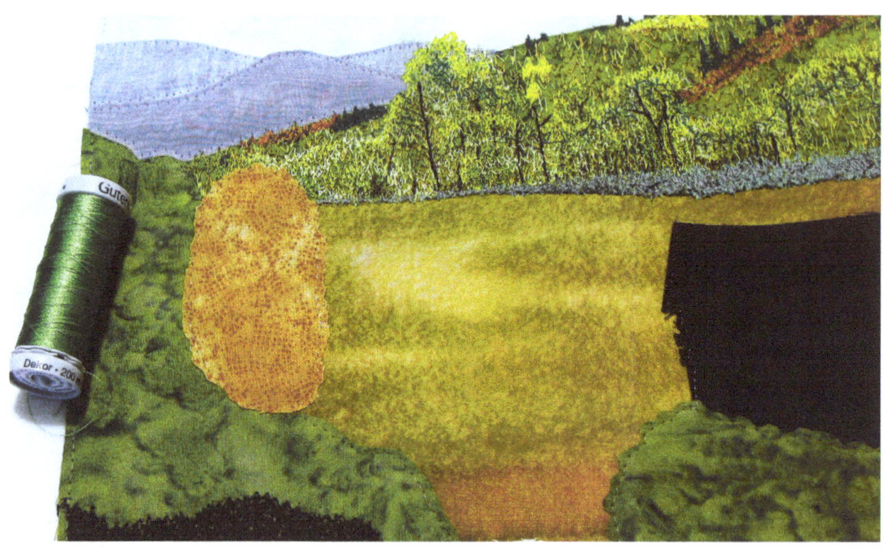

Now I'll go in and put some green stitching for the trees on the left. Then some yellow-green, again using the random zigzag stitch.

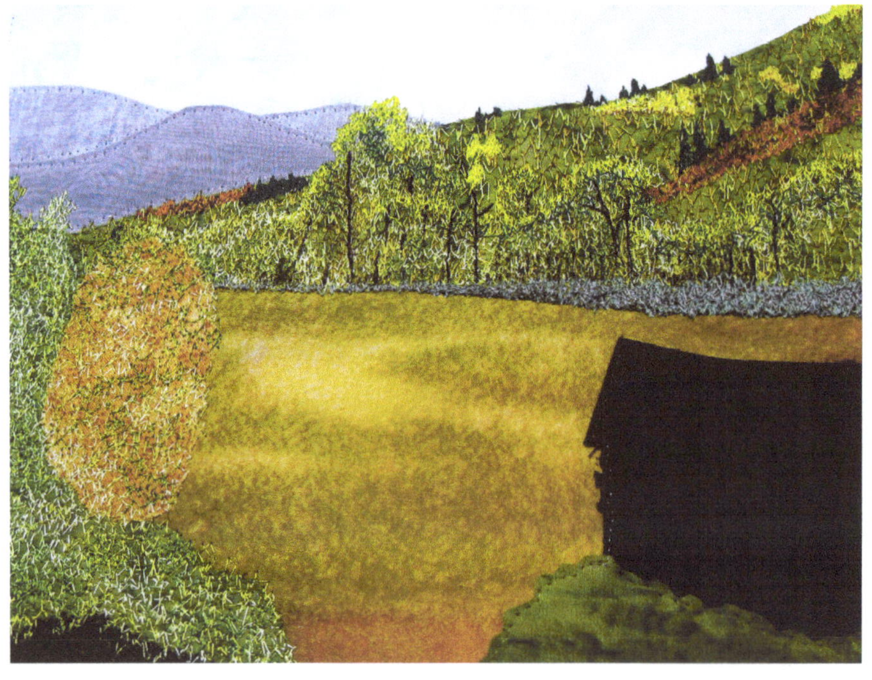

Notice how the fabric seems to have changed colors just by using a lighter colored thread. You can do the same thing by using a darker thread to change the look of your fabrics.

I need to define the trees more. So I'm going to go ahead and draw in their trunks and branches. That will make it easier for me to define each tree with some bright yellow thread.

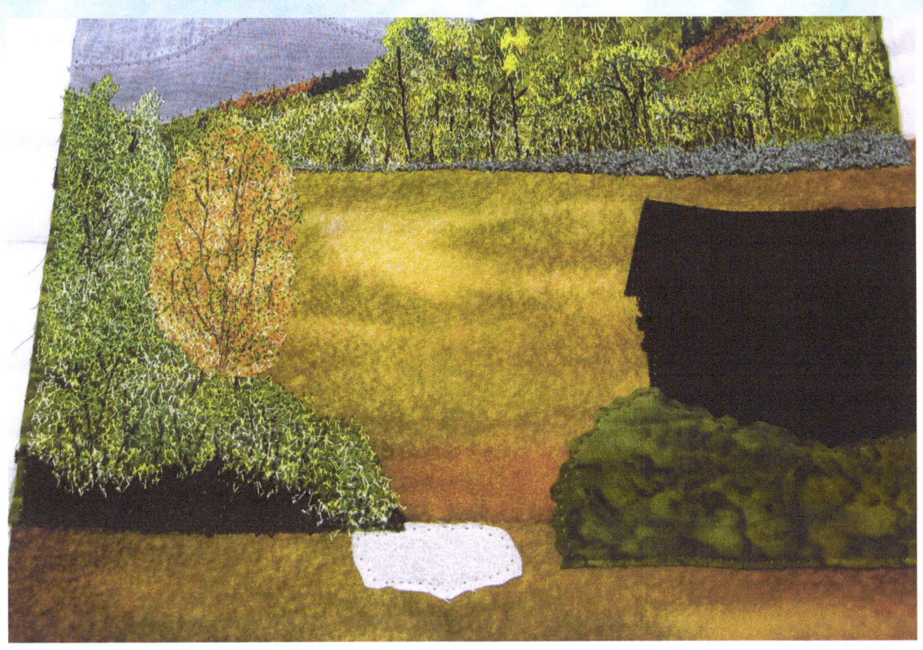

As I put my picture and photo on my design wall, I see that I need to fill in the shadow some more. I'll do that with a black marker. I don't want to cover up my stitching, so I dot the area rather than fill it in. By using dots, I better control the shading and ensure that my colored stitches don't get covered up. It also provides a more textured look .

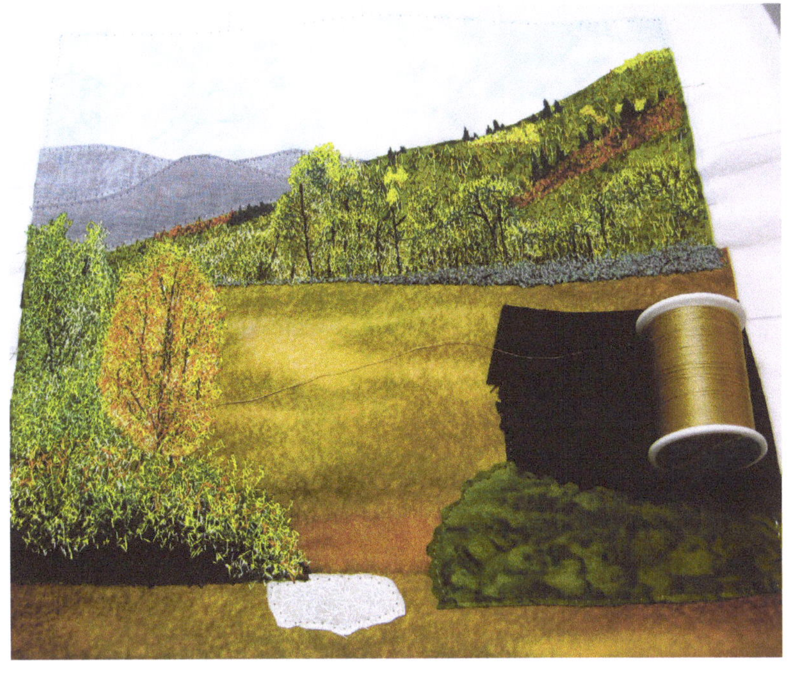

Now I'm going to add the stitching for the lighter grasses in the middle-ground field. My fabric has some highlighted areas, so I'm going to bring out those areas with the thread. I'm going to continue using the random zigzag stitch.

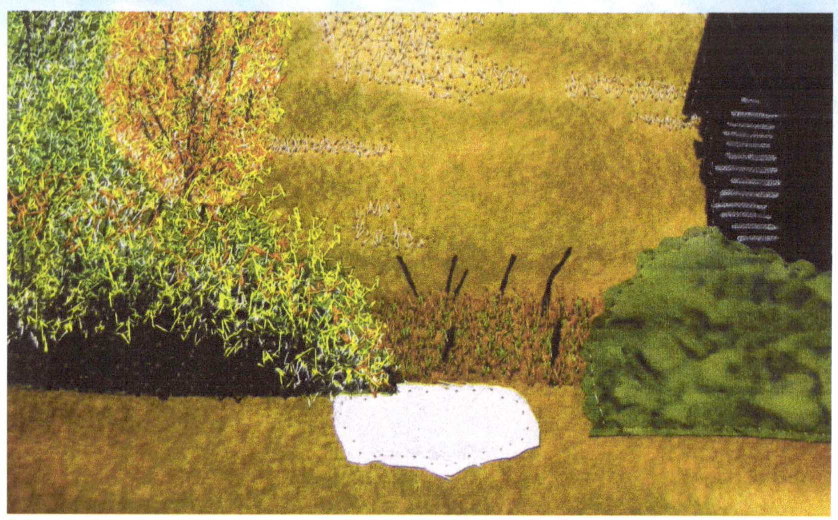

Now I'll make the green grass between the bushes near the creek and cabin yard. Then I can draw in the fence posts, and add some brownish grass to overlap the fence posts a bit.

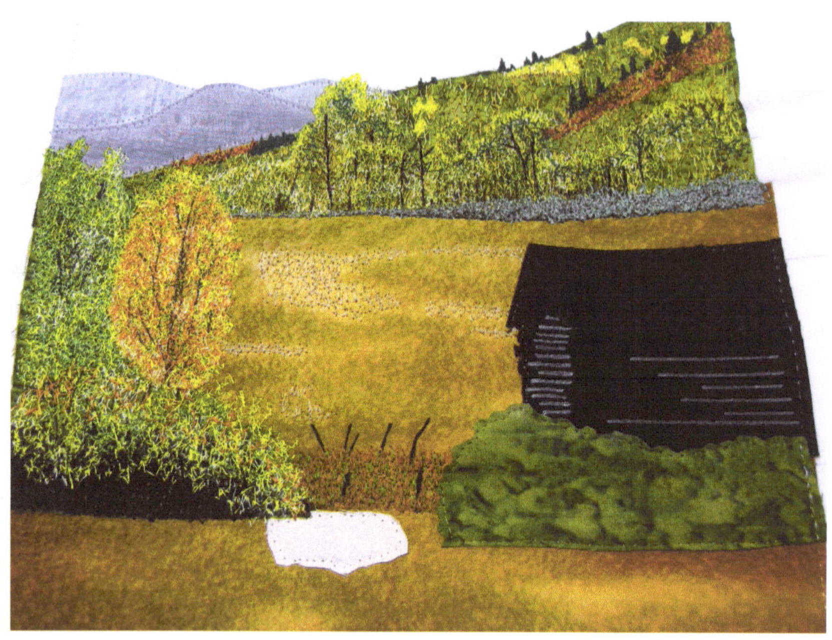

Now it's time to tackle the cabin. Using scraps of the cabin fabric, I'll do some experimenting with different pens, paints and threads to get the look I want. Using a quilters pencil, I'll draw the outline of the roof and logs. I'm going to use the silver Sharpie to draw the log highlights. Then I'm going to use a dark pen to do more detailing.

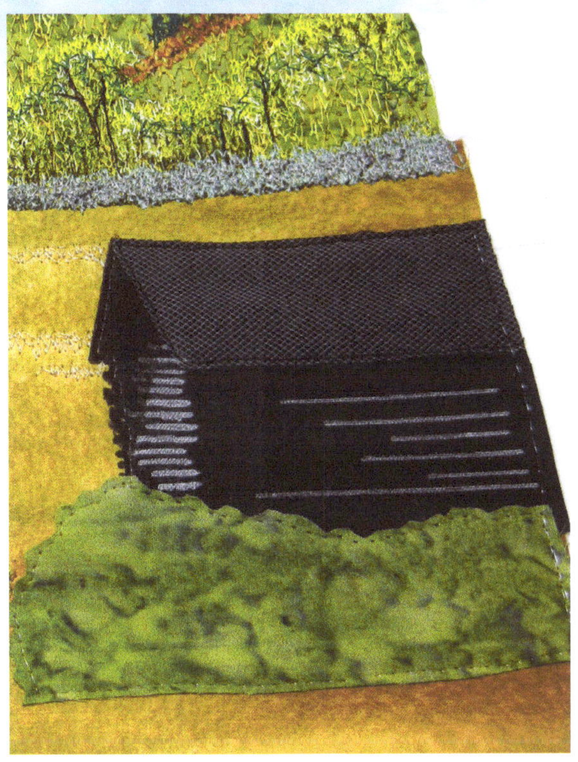

For the shingles, I'm going to put a layer of off-white bridal tulle on the cabin roof. To do that, I'll use dark brown thread and a straight stitch to apply it to the roof. Then using rounded tipped scissors, trim the excess tulle off, similar to how I put the organza over the mountains to make them look hazy.

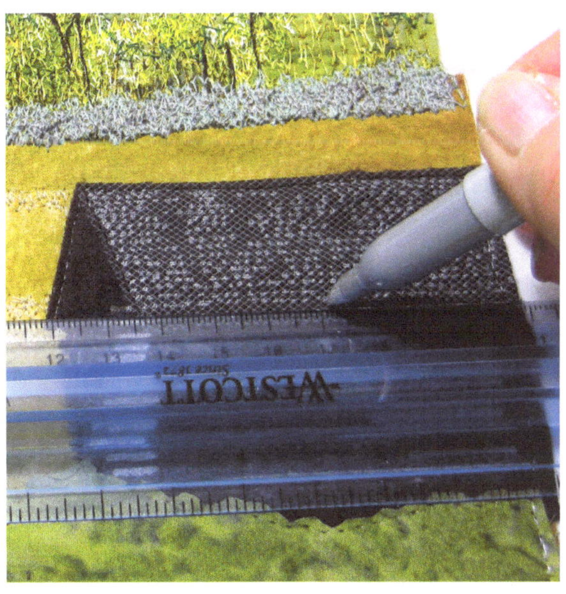

Next, using the silver Sharpie, I'll "dot" some shingles in. Then I use a black Sharpie to darken in the shadow at the peak of the roof. I'm also going to use a straight stitch and sew along the lines of some of the logs. Later, when the picture is almost done, I plan to go in with some white fabric paint and put some highlights on the logs. That will brighten them up a bit.

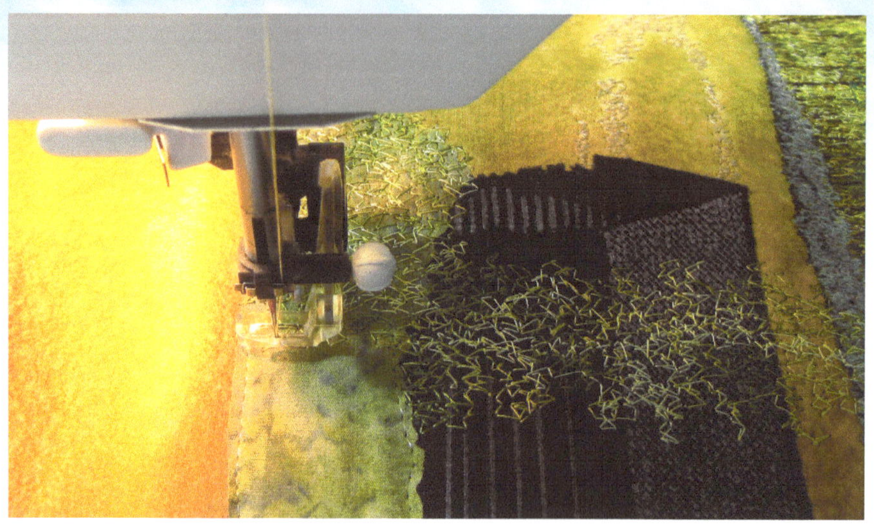

TIP

I used a Quilters pencil and drew the tree trunk and some branches. That will be my guide for stitching the leaves in the tree.

Now I'll stitch the large yellow tree and bushes in front of the cabin. Again I'll use the zigzag stitch and move the canvas around randomly to get the leaves. I'm going to be very careful not to rip the tulle on the roof.

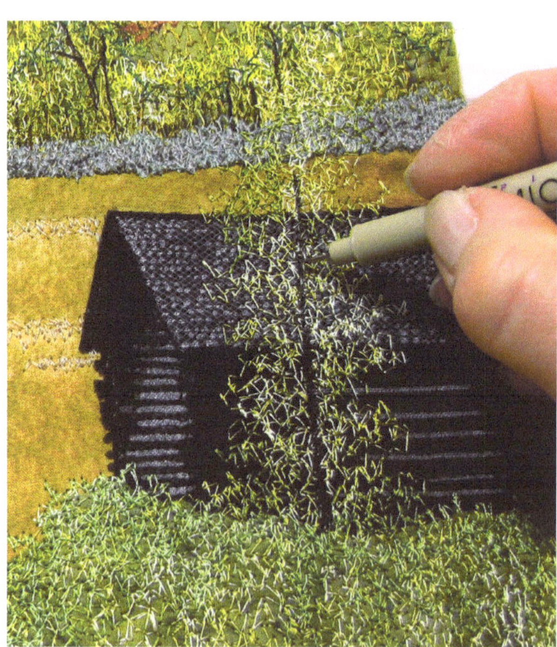

After filling in the bushes and tree, I'm going to use a dark brown marker and draw in the trunk of the tree and some branches. Then I'll go in with some bright yellow thread and fill in some more leaves.

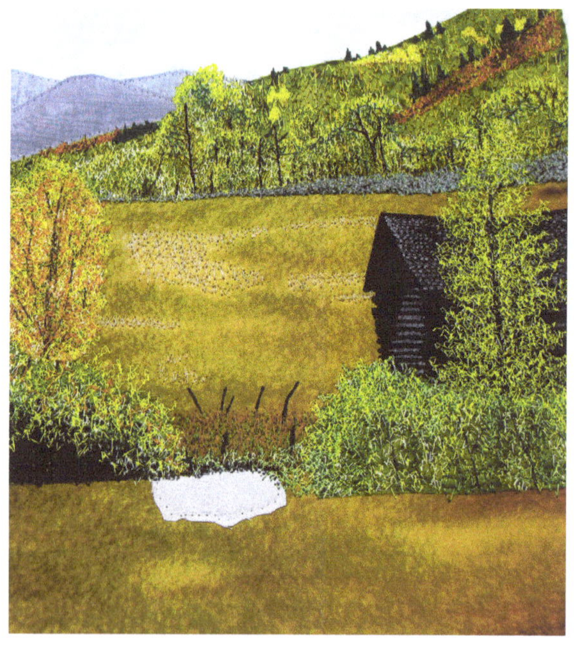

After filling in the bushes and tree, I'm going to use a dark brown marker and draw in the trunk of the tree and some branches. Then I'll go in with some bright yellow thread and fill in some more leaves.

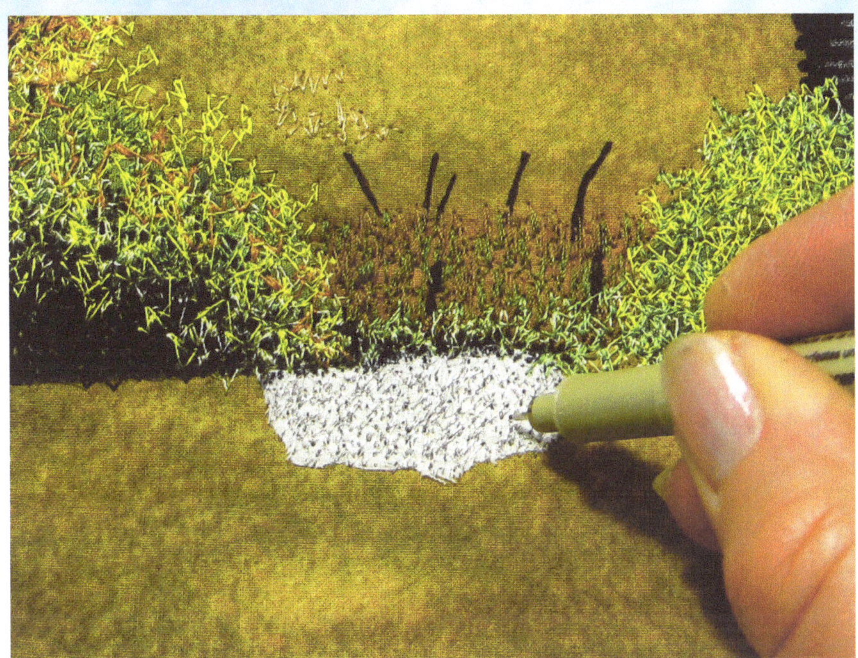

I'll fill the water in with the random zigzag stitches and silver metallic thread. And then I'll go in with a fine tipped marker and make some darker areas to give it more depth.

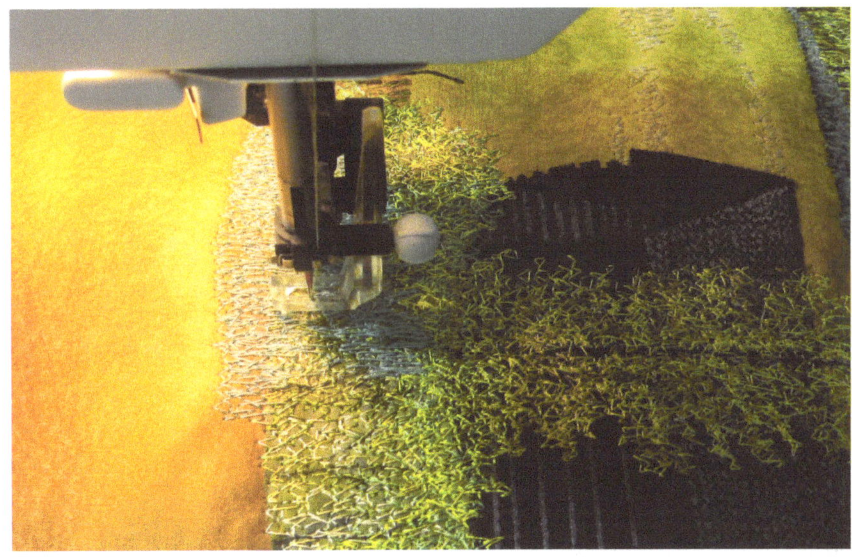

Now I'll work on the sagebrush in front of the bushes on the right side of the picture. I want them to be the same colors and blend well with the sagebrush that is in front of the big hill. To accomplish this, I'll use the same colors and technique. I'll just make bigger stitches.

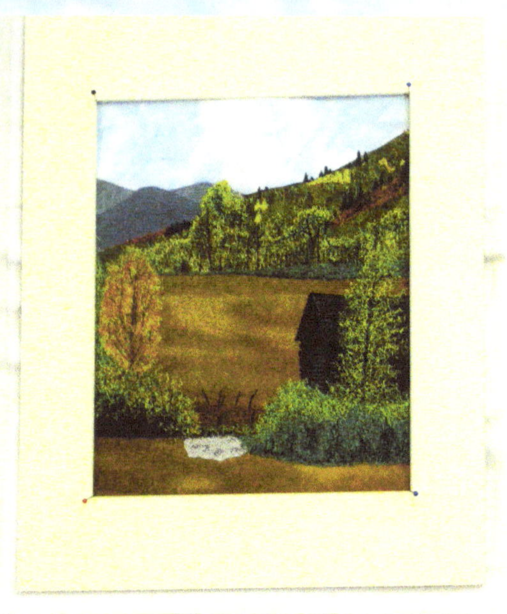
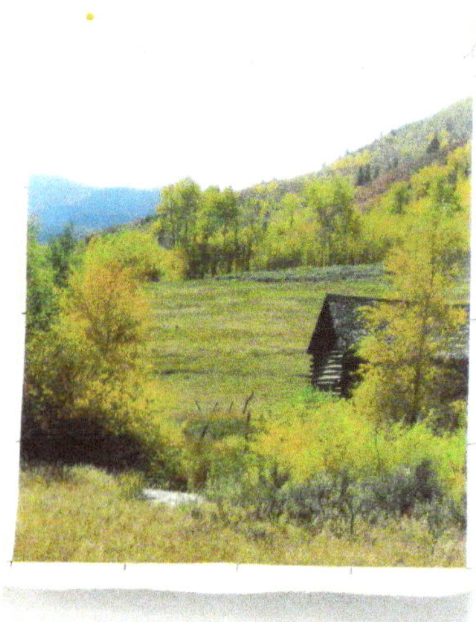

I drew some of the branches in the sagebrush. Now I want to step back and take a look at it and see if I need to add anything. I pinned the matt board over my picture to see how it looks so far.

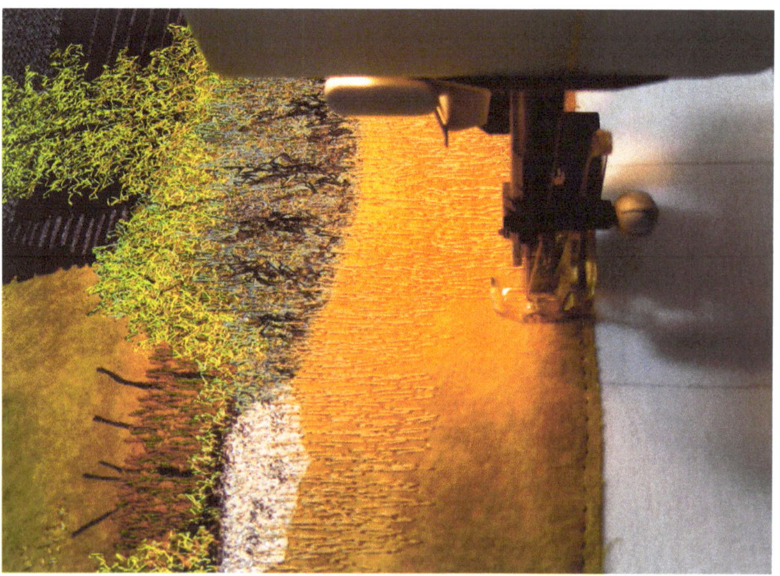

I'm going to stitch the grasses in the foreground with the same color thread I used for the field grasses. I'm going to use the zigzag stitch, but move my canvas up and down more to make longer stitches. Notice that I'm still working perpendicular to the picture.

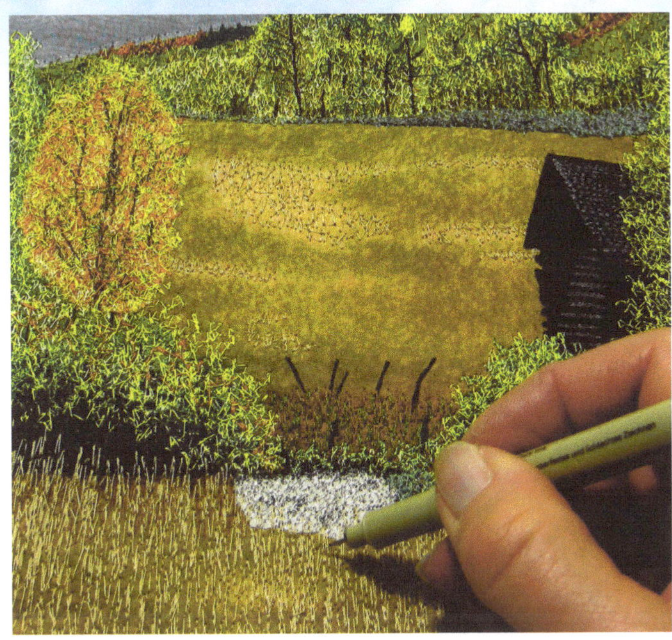

Once I have the grasses in, I could still see a definite line between the large shadow on the left, and the grasses. So I went in with a medium brown marker and used small up and down lines to blend the two together. Now I'm going over the grasses with another variegated thread and darker brown thread to blend everything some more. I'm going to keep working on blending the two areas until I get the look that I'm after.

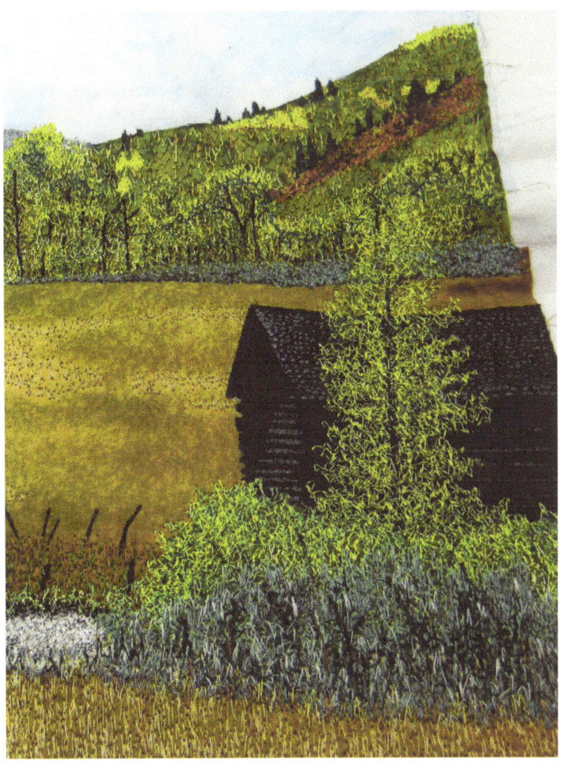

I'm now going to go in and put some highlights on the log cabin using white fabric paint.

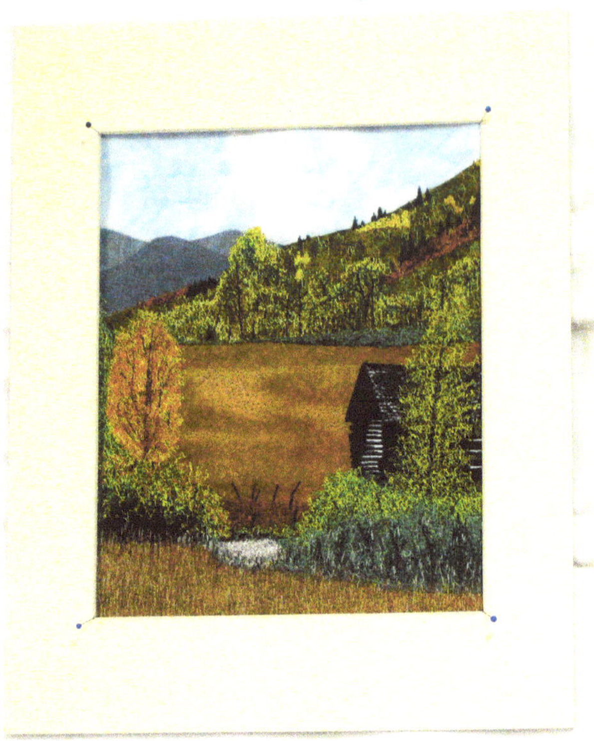

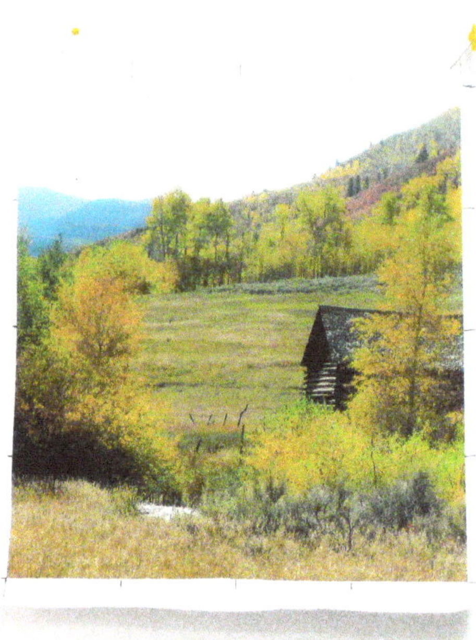

Once you've completed your embellishing, put it on your design wall or easel and stand back and look at it. Compare it to your inspirational photo. Do you need a lighter or darker shade of thread added to give it more depth in any area? Sometimes you can go in and add some shading with a permanent pen or marker. You will also notice that your canvas is getting quite stiff and harder to sew on by this time.

Your embellishing has caused your canvas to "pull together." That is one reason you want to have about equal interest in all areas of your picture. Your picture will pull together more evenly that way. By covering the sky with netting and using invisible thread to sew wavy random lines, (as described in Chapter 6) you will pull the sky together a little to help balance out the pulling on the more detailed portions of your canvas. This pulling together is the reason why we marked our canvas ½ inch outside of the mat board opening. You want to make sure your mat board opening will cover the edges of your finished piece.

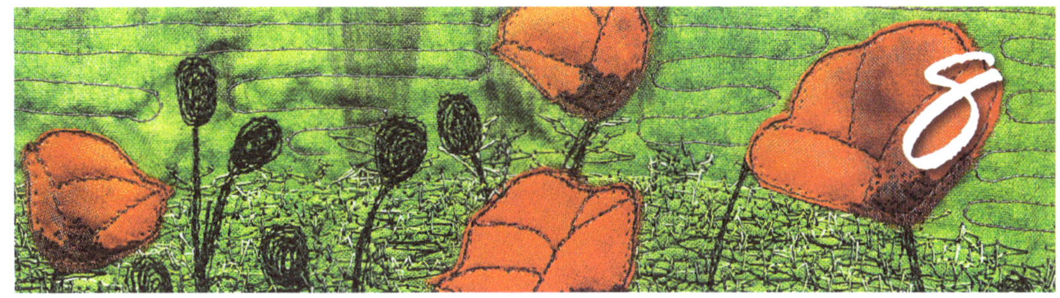

Finishing your Artwork

When you are happy with your picture, it's time to think about framing it. I like using a double mat board on my pieces. It gives them a nice professional look. And since you used a standard precut mat board when preparing your canvas, you can easily find a variety of precut double mat boards to choose from at your local arts or crafts store.

Once you've decided on your mat board, center it over your piece and see if there's an area on your artwork where you can sign and date it.

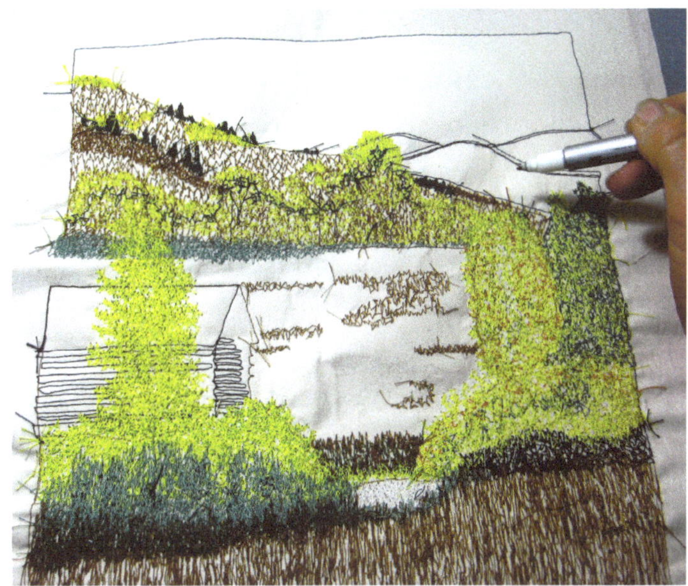

Sometimes there's so much embellishing that it makes it hard to do. In that case, be sure you sign the back of your piece in a place that won't show through your canvas.

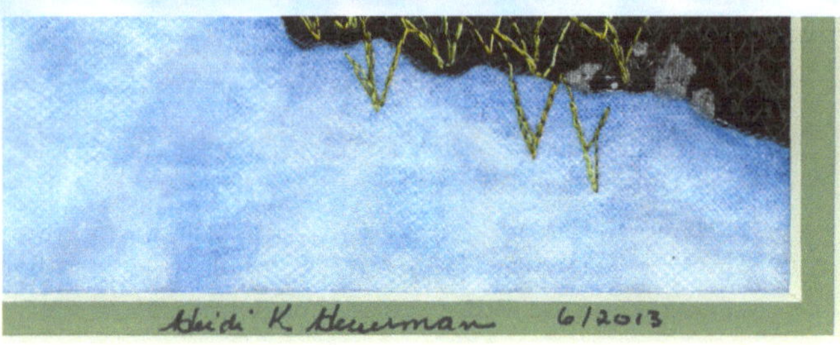

And then sign and date the front of your mat board. I often sign and date my pieces on the inside mat, close to the bottom right corner.

Put a strip of double-sided tape around the backside of your mat board opening. I usually put it about 1/8" from the opening, all the way around.

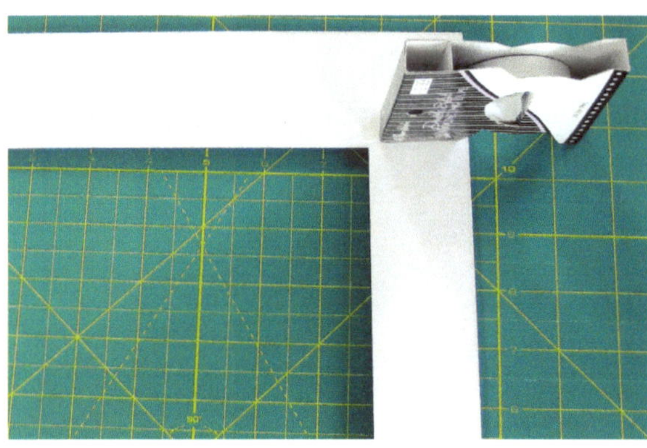

Lay your art piece on a flat, clean surface. Carefully place your mat board, with the double-stick tape, over the canvas, centering your embellished artwork. Press the edges of the mat board firmly onto your canvas. Flip it over and carefully pull and stretch your canvas to pull out as many puckers as possible. Again, press firmly with your hands to get the tape to stick well to your canvas. Trim the canvas around your picture, leaving as much canvas as possible.

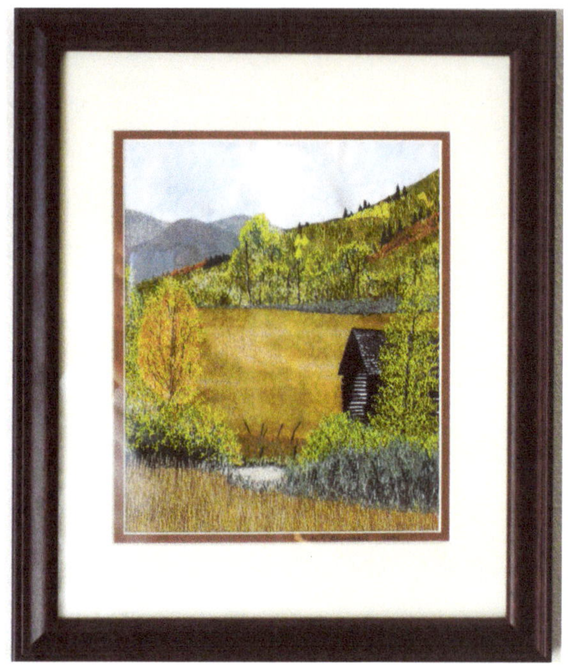

At this point you can frame it yourself or take it somewhere to get it framed. I almost always use glass in my frames. It protects the fabrics from becoming dusty and dirty. And remember, don't hang your new art in direct sunlight. It will fade.

Congratulation! You've completed a unique, three-dimensional fiber painting!

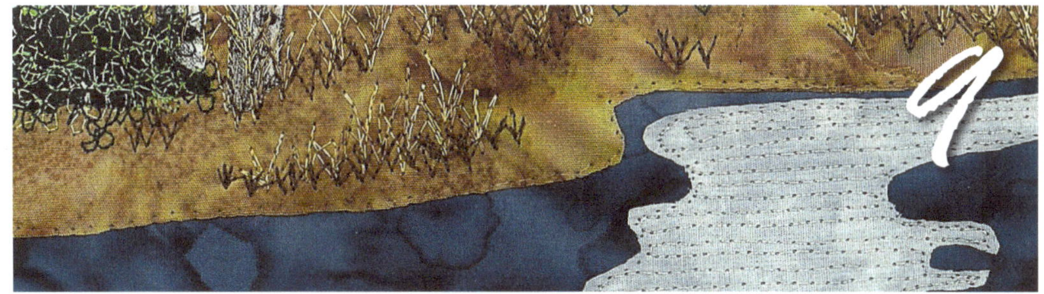

Gallery of Fiber Paintings

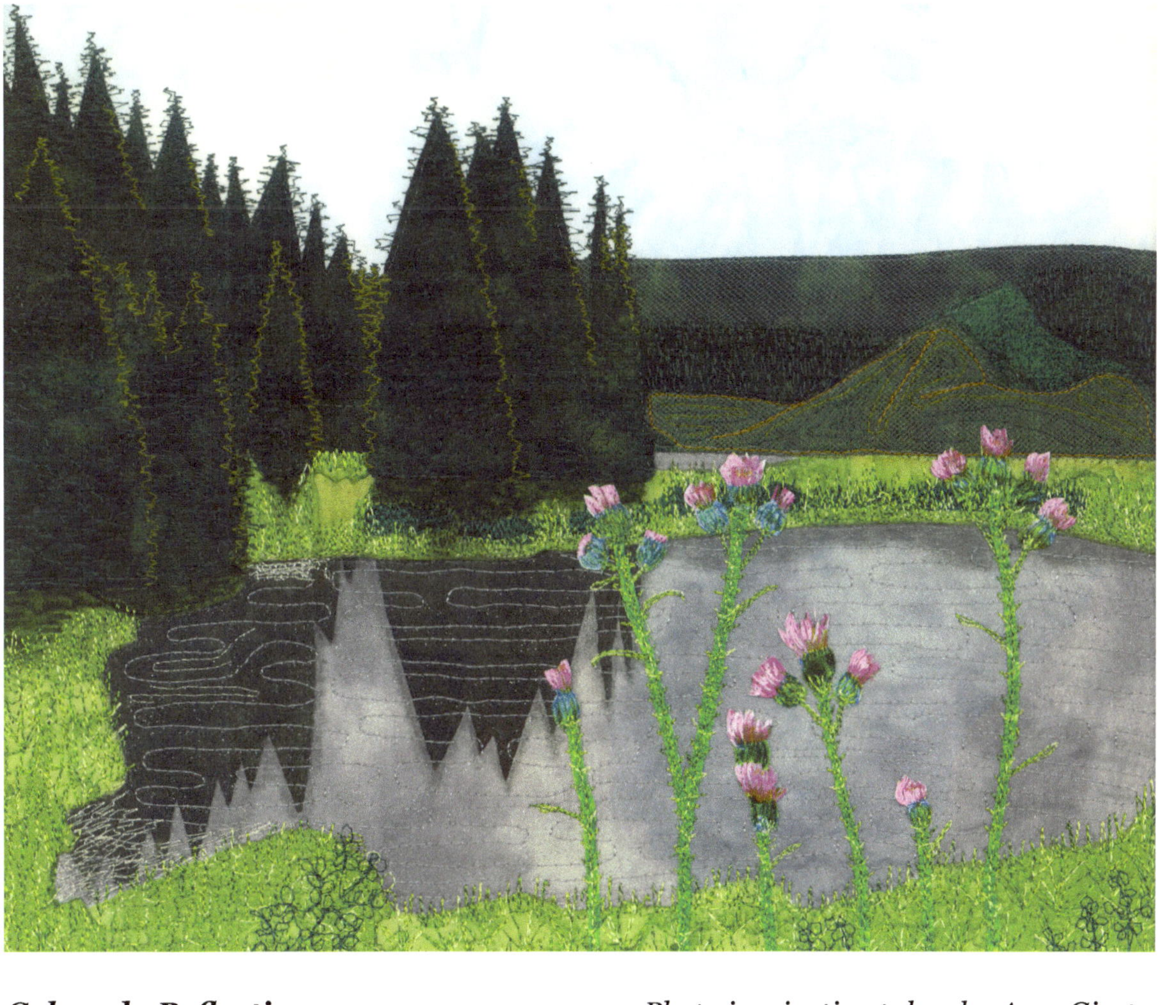

Colorado Reflections *Photo inspiration taken by Amy Giertz*

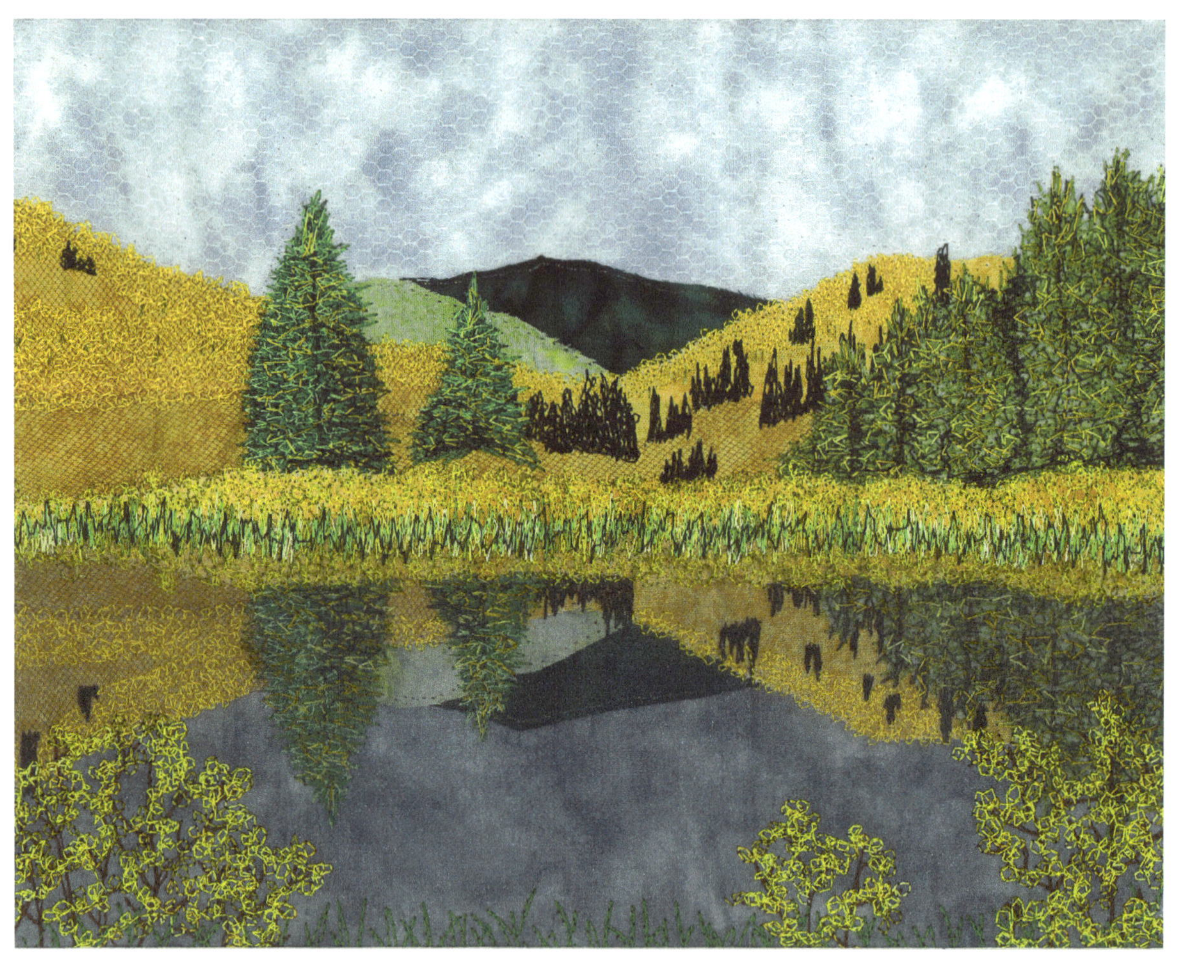

Autumn Is Here *Photo inspiration taken by Amy Giertz*

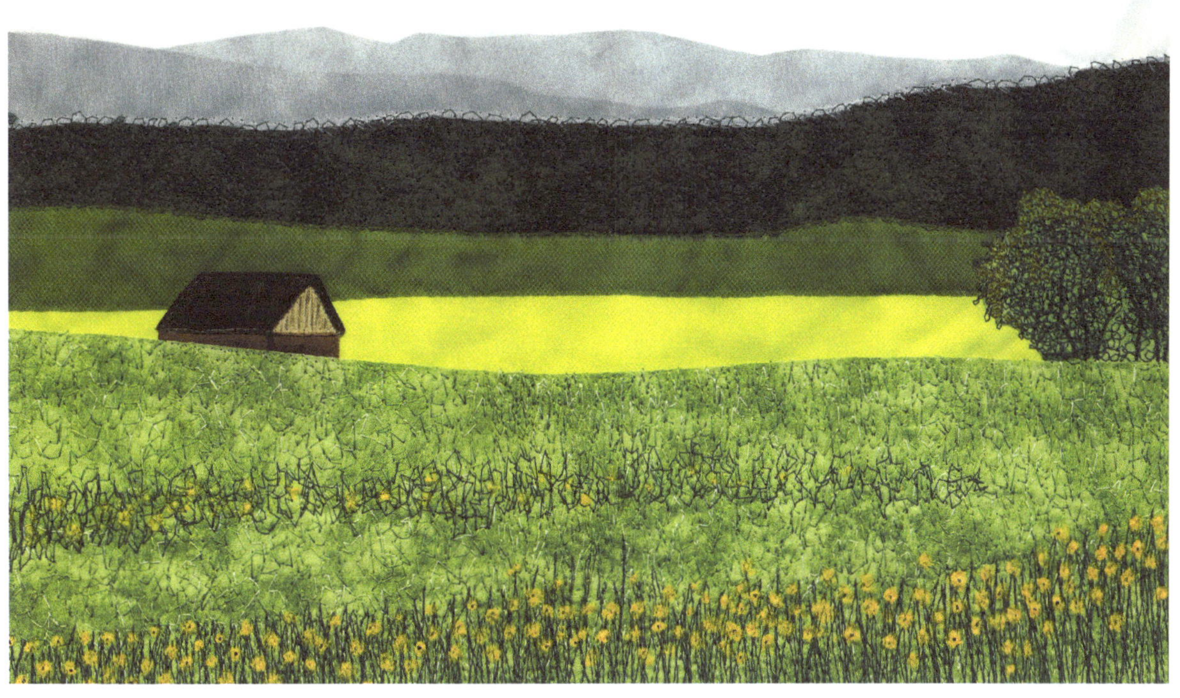

Sunlit Field *Photo inspiration taken by Amy Giertz*

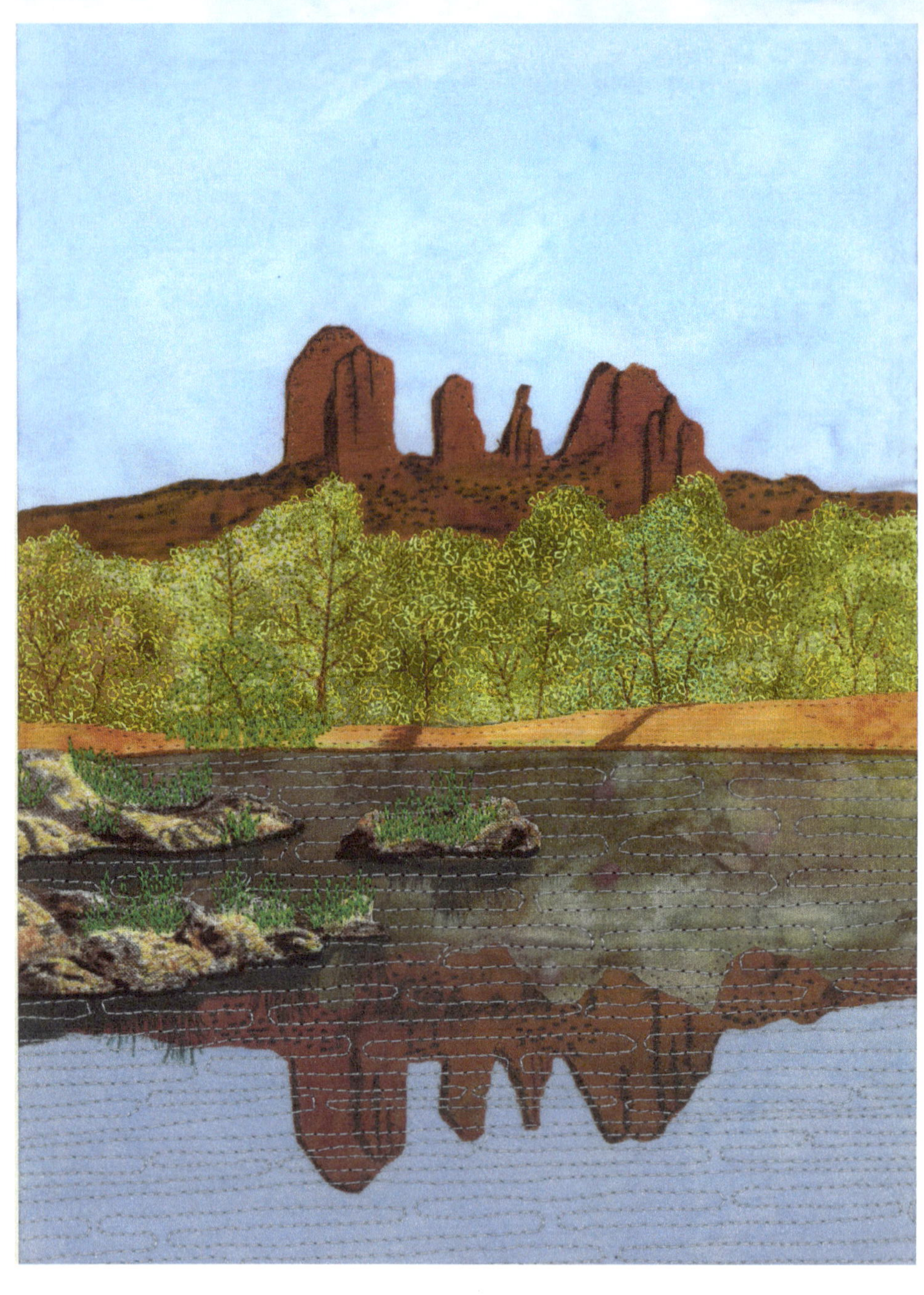

Arizona Afternoon *Inspiration from unidentified calendar photo*

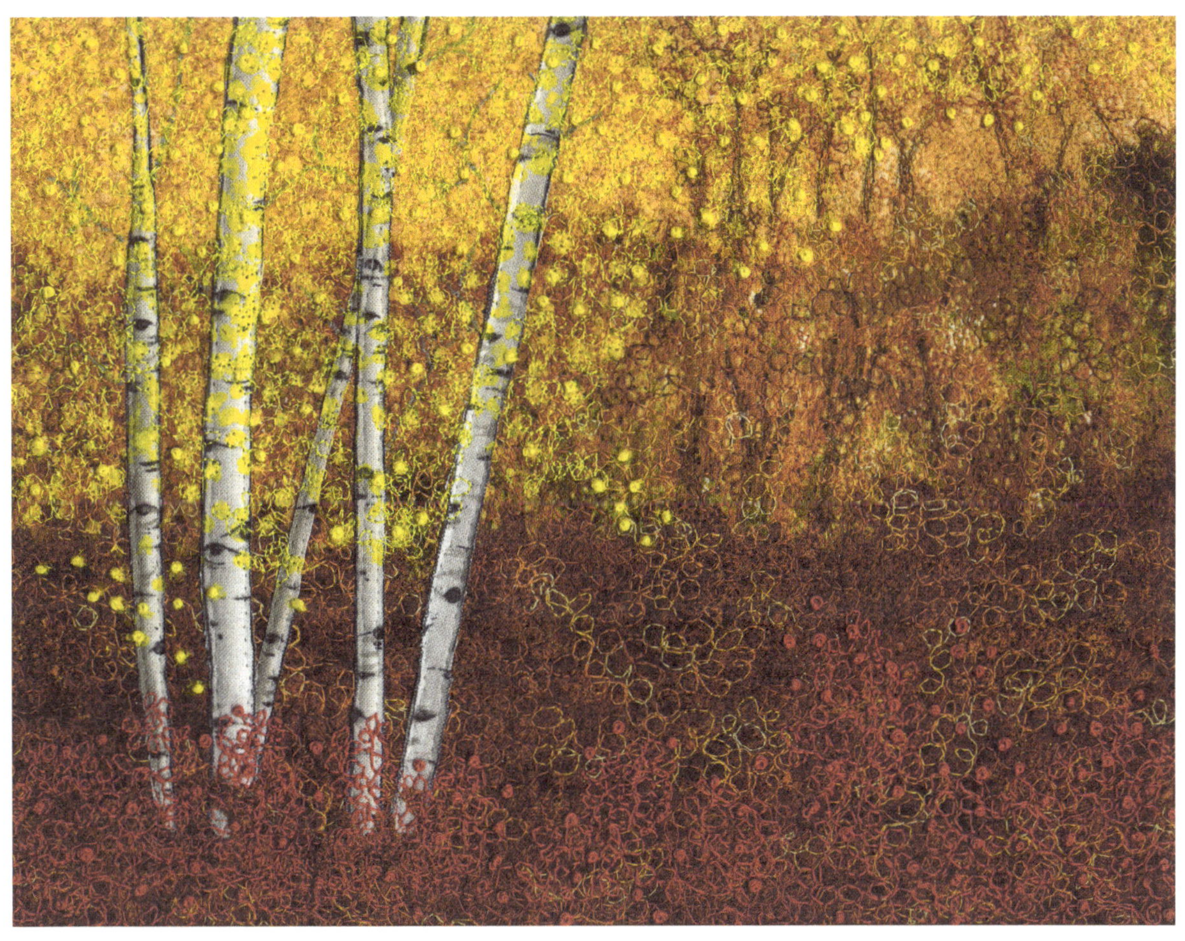

Birches *Inspiration from a neighbor's yard*

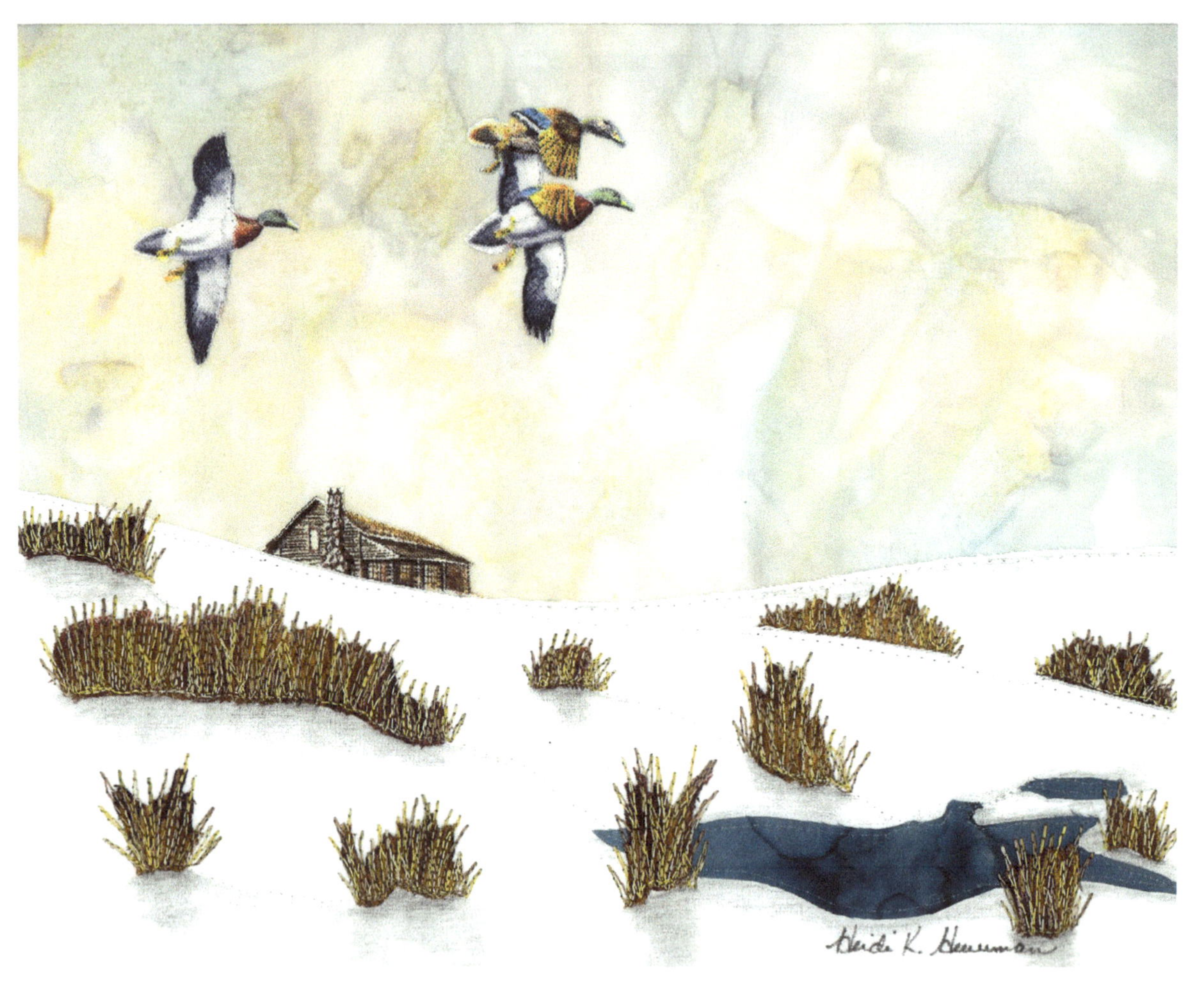

Coming of Winter *Inspiration from memories of Wyoming*

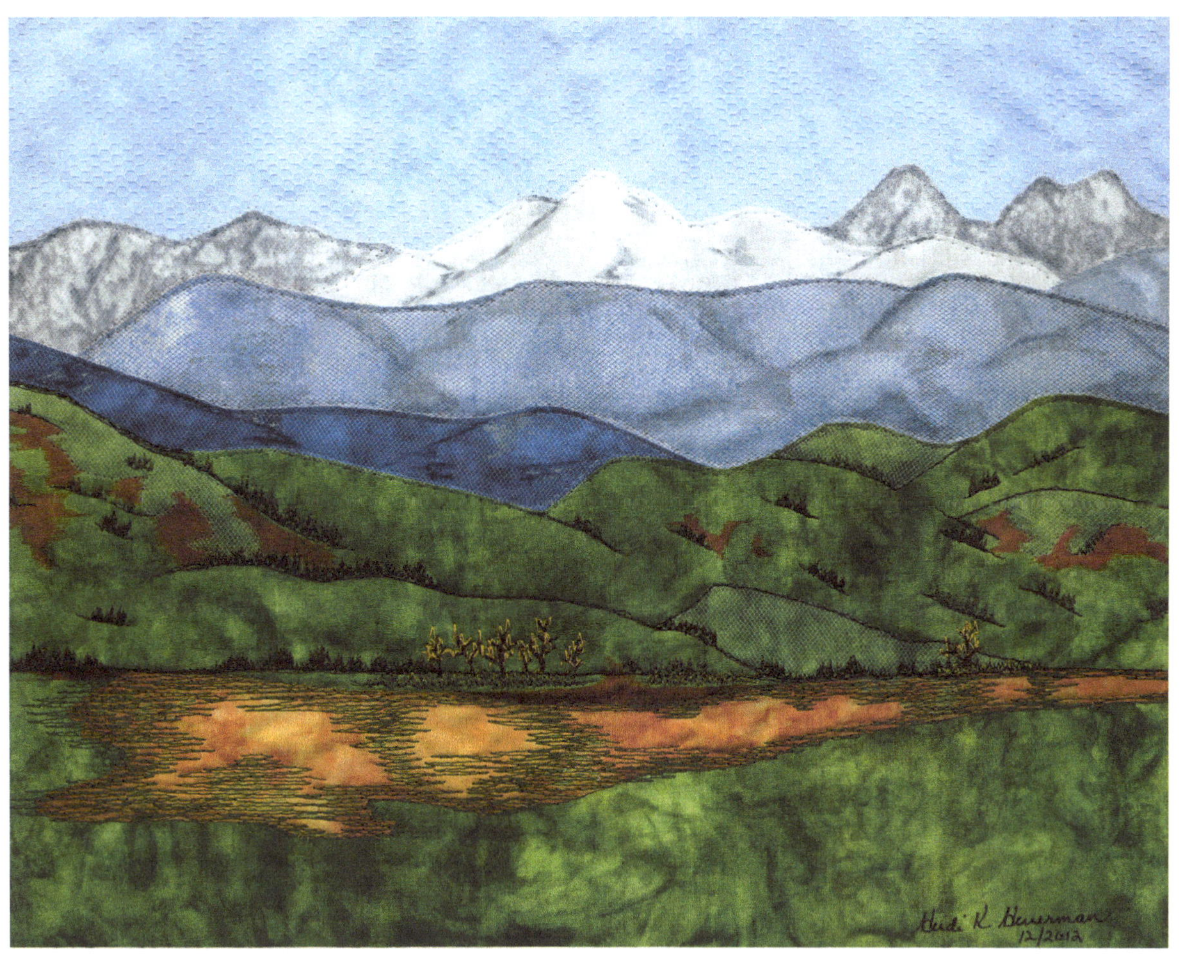

Scoria *Inspiration from driving through Northeastern Wyoming*

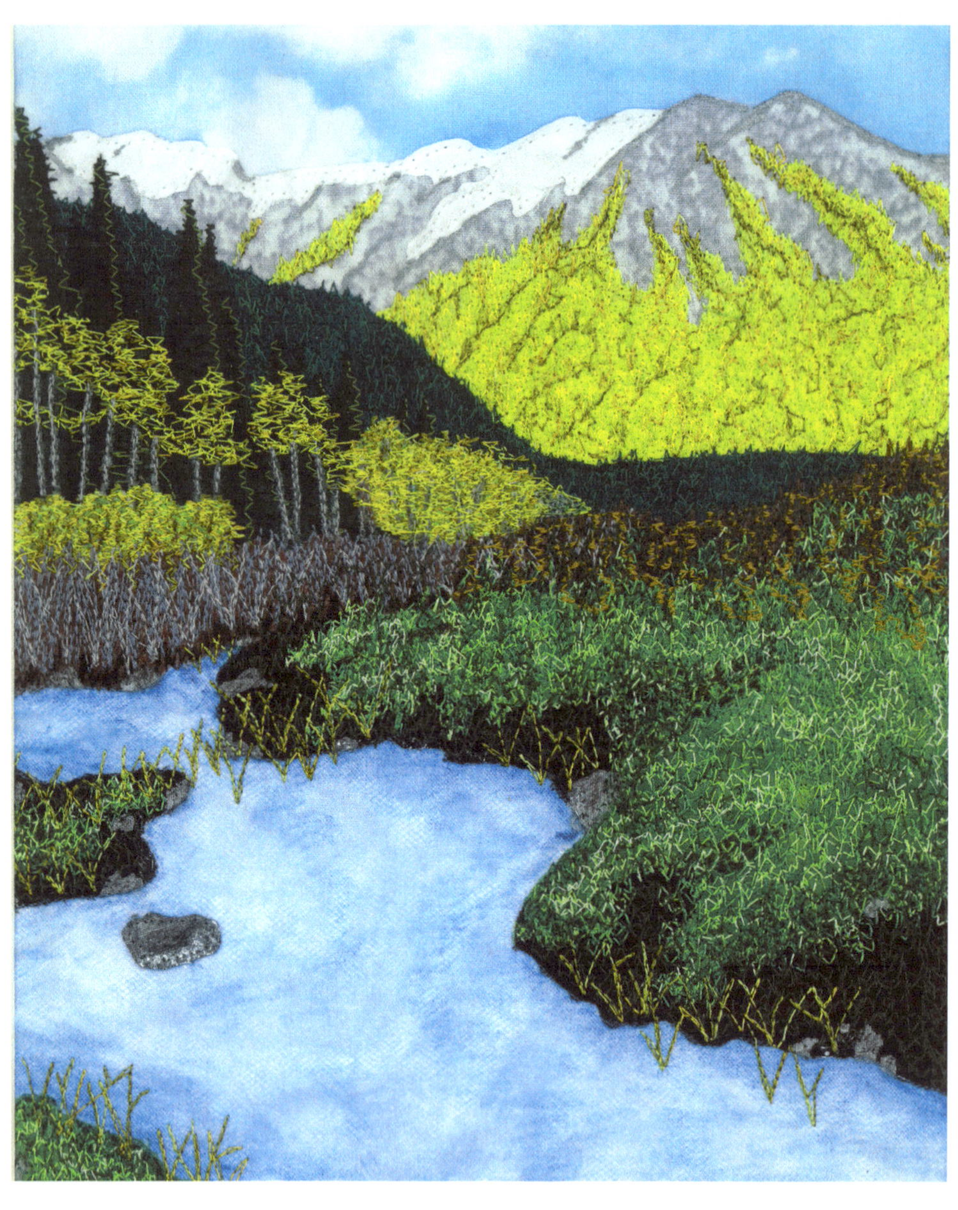

Spring Thaw *Inspiration from the Colorado Rocky Mountains*

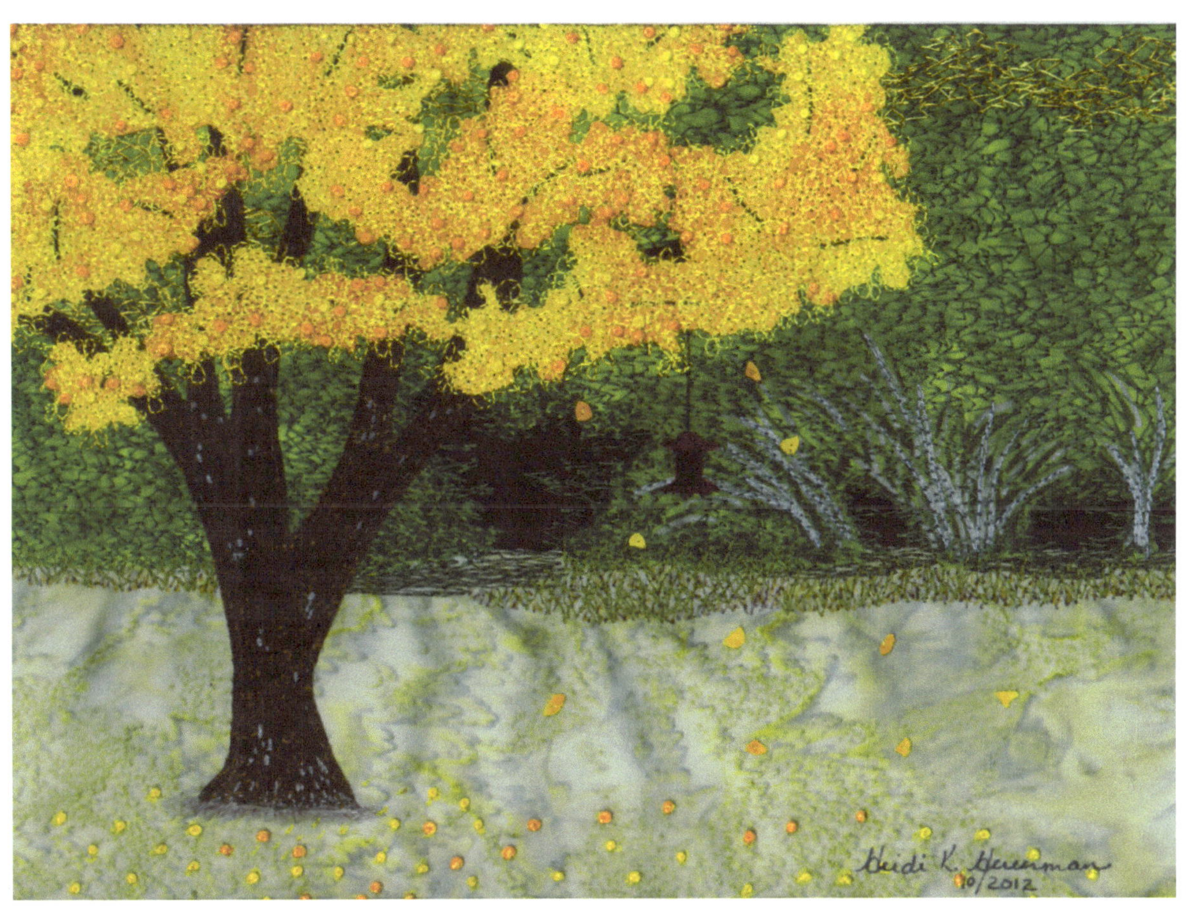

Backyard Tree *Inspiration from our backyard in October*

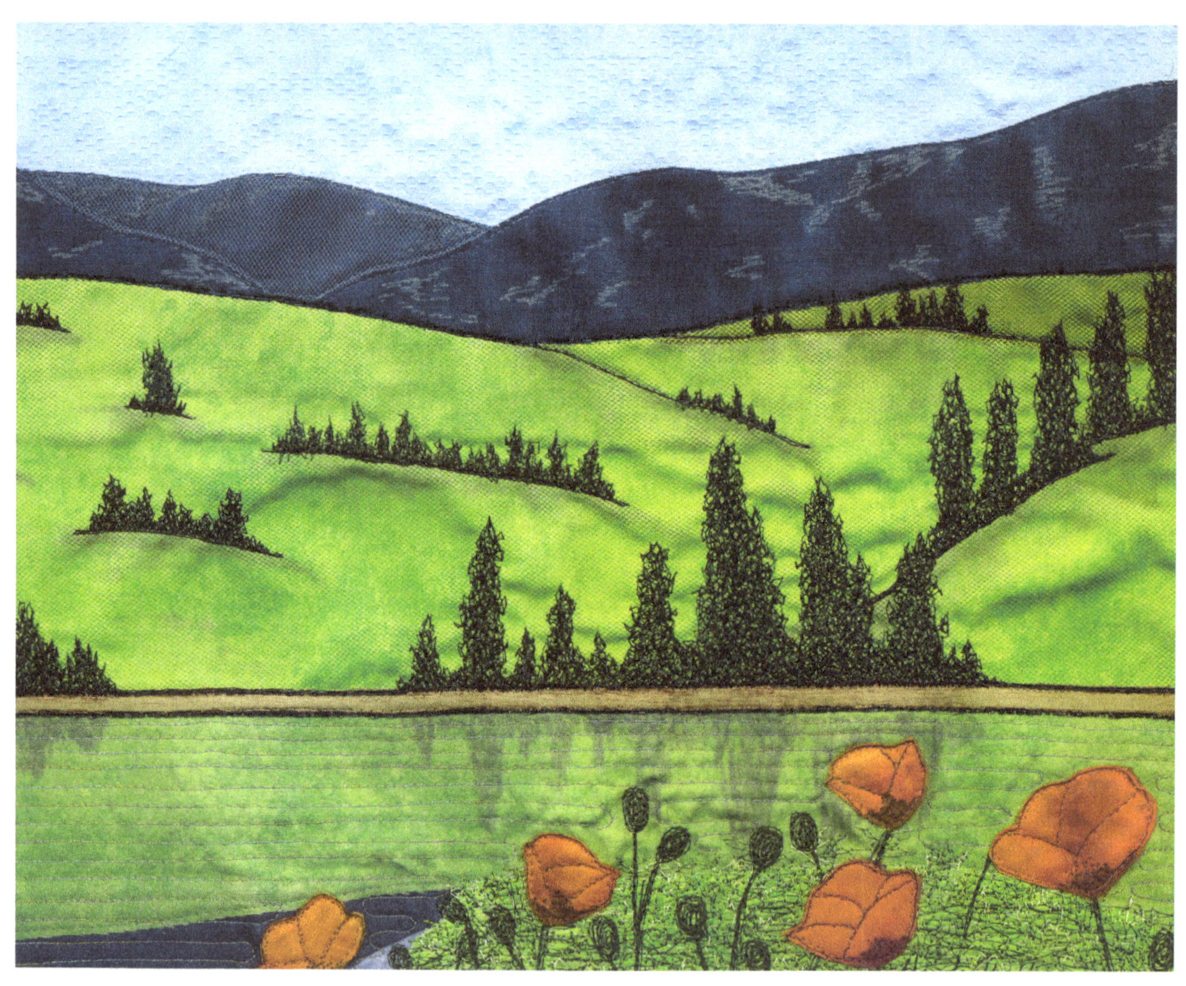

Poppies by the Pond *Inspiration from the foothills of Wyoming*

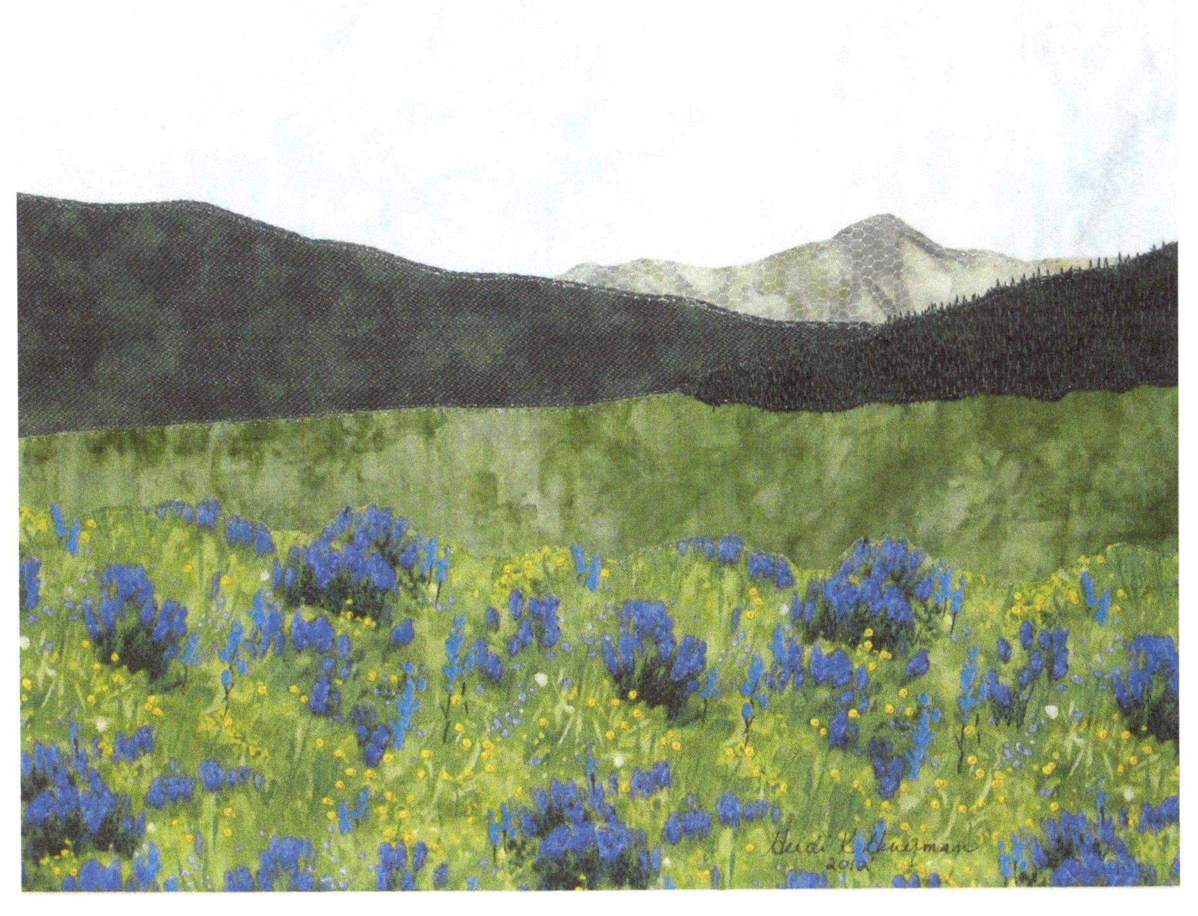

Big Horn Meadow *Inspiration from the Big Horn Mountains of Wyoming*

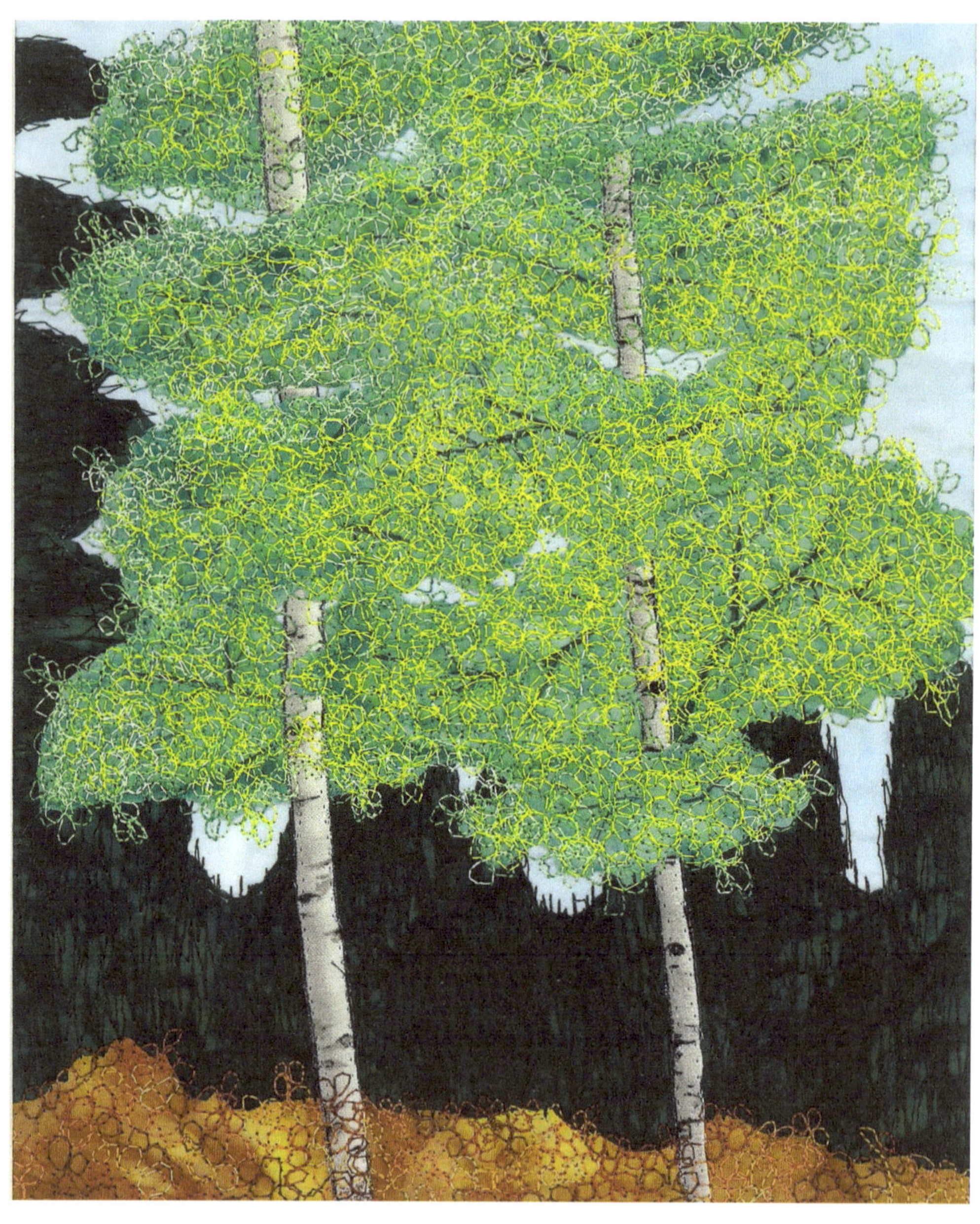

Aspens *Inspiration from the Big Horn Mountains of Wyoming*

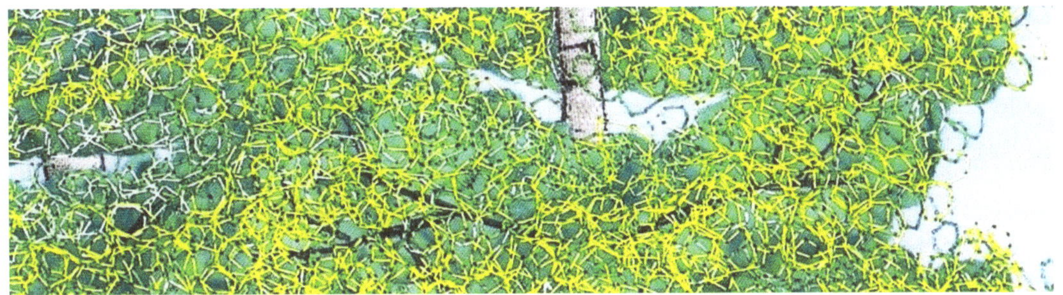

Online Resources

See Heidi's website, www.HeidisArtEmporium.com, to purchase kits for various pictures and to see her latest creations.

Computer Fabric Sheets called Printed Treasures

- Available at most quilt shops
- Hobby Lobby, www.hobbylobby.com
- Jo-Ann Fabrics, www.joann.com

Fabrics

- Batiks Galore, www.Batiksgalore.com
- Fabric.Com, www.Fabric.com
- Quilter's Quarters, www.Quiltersqtrs.com
- Skydyes, www.Skydyes.com

Mat Board

- Available at various stores including Hobby Lobby and Michaels

Notions and Fabrics

- Nancy's Notions, www.Nancysnotions.com
- Superior Threads, www.superiorthreads.com

Fabric Starch

- Mary Ellen's Products, Inc., www.maryellenproducts.com

505 Fabric Adhesive

- Jo-Ann Fabrics, www.joann.com

www.ingramcontent.com/pod-product-compliance
Lightning Source LLC
LaVergne TN
LVHW070144110826
845147LV00002B/327
9780692201206